The Rise of the Green Left

Inside the Worldwide Ecosocialist Movement

Derek Wall

Foreword by
Hugo Blanco

PlutoPress
www.plutobooks.com

First published 2010 by Pluto Press
345 Archway Road, London N6 5AA and
175 Fifth Avenue, New York, NY 10010

www.plutobooks.com

Distributed in the United States of America exclusively by
Palgrave Macmillan, a division of St. Martin's Press LLC,
175 Fifth Avenue, New York, NY 10010

British Library Cataloguing in Publication Data
A catalogue record for this book is available from the British Library

ISBN   978 0 7453 3037 2   Hardback
ISBN   978 0 7453 3036 5   Paperback

Library of Congress Cataloging in Publication Data applied for

This book is printed on paper suitable for recycling and made from
fully managed and sustained forest sources. Logging, pulping and
manufacturing processes are expected to conform to the environmental
standards of the country of origin.

10   9   8   7   6   5   4   3   2   1

Designed and produced for Pluto Press by
Chase Publishing Services Ltd, 33 Livonia Road, Sidmouth, EX10 9JB, England
Typeset from disk by Stanford DTP Services, Northampton, England
Printed and bound in the European Union by
CPI Antony Rowe, Chippenham and Eastbourne

To Sarah Farrow

Even an entire society, a nation, or all simultaneously existing societies taken together, are not the owners of the earth. They are simply its possessors, its beneficiaries, and have to bequeath it in an improved state to succeeding generations as *boni patres familias* [good heads of the household].

Marx 1981: 911 (http://tiny.cc/xrHUv)

I was reading about the reasons for the disappearance of song birds in Germany. The spread of scientific forestry, horticulture, and agriculture, have cut them off from their nesting places and their food supply. More and more, with modern methods, we are doing away with hollow trees, waste lands, brushwood, fallen leaves. I felt sore at heart. I was not thinking so much about the loss of pleasure for human beings, but I was so much distressed at the idea of the stealthy and inexorable destruction of these defenceless little creatures, that the tears came into my eyes.

Letter from Rosa Luxemburg to Sophie Liebknecht, 2 May 1917 (http://tiny.cc/TfMi5).

Contents

Acknowledgements

Thanks to Farid Bakht, Hugo Blanco, Oscar Blanco Berglund, Owen Clayton, Dave Costain, Kadir Dadan, Klaus Engert, Jonathan Essex, Sarah Farrow, Phil Gasper, Lesley Hedges, Michael Löwy, Dan Murray, Pete Murry, Pablo Navarrete, Sarah Parker, Gareth Price-Thomas, Dave Riley, Ignacio Sabbatella, Matt Sellwood, Alex Snowdon, Alan Thornett and José Antonio Vergara. And of course to Dave Castle as editor. All of you helped me, the mistakes, though, are all mine.

Foreword

Hugo Blanco

This book clearly and conclusively shows the incompatibility between the capitalist system and the protection of the environment. The capitulation of many green parties to capitalism has converted them into anti-ecologists.

The book also highlights the fact that in today's world it is impossible to have a coherent socialism which does not incorporate ecology. In this respect, we see how the Ecuadorian government, which has been put forward as one of the practitioners of 'twenty-first-century socialism', has surrendered to the idea that nature is there for us to exploit. This has led to a confrontation with Ecuador's indigenous population, who are defending the environment.

The book shows us once again that if humanity remains being led by the big multinational corporations, the direct result will be the liquidation of the human species, in the same way that we have already exterminated many other species.

Another aspect worth highlighting is Derek's observation that 'The most important area of discussion must be how can we stop the train before it leaps the rails. The question of how ecosocialists fight for change is the one we must ask and re-ask.'

Further along Derek tells us: 'The political system has been better at changing radicals than the radicals have been at changing the system.' With responsible prudence, he points out that 'This chapter examines strategy and makes some suggestions, it does not claim to provide "the answer"; however, if it encourages discussion which leads to focused and effective action, it will have achieved something.'

Further on, Derek talks about the struggle of indigenous peoples in defending the environment, including the case of Bagua, Peru.

I should point out that this focus on indigenous struggle is not just of theoretical interest to Derek. He shows solidarity in practice and has organised and promoted many events in support of not only Bagua, but also indigenous peoples around the world.

He calls attention to the words of Elinor Ostrom, the 2009 Nobel laureate in Economics:

> Our problem is how to craft rules at multiple levels that enable humans to adapt, learn, and change over time so that we are sustaining the very valuable natural resources that we inherited so that we may be able to pass them on. I am deeply indebted to the indigenous peoples in the U.S. who had an image of seven generations being the appropriate time to think about the future. I think we should all reinstate in our mind the seven-generation rule. When we make really major decisions, we should ask not only what will it do for me today, but what will it do for my children, my children's children, and their children's children into the future.

It is significant that he has asked me to write this foreword, rather than a distinguished academic. He sees me as one of the representatives of the indigenous struggle.

In Europe, the concept of a socialist society existed long before Marx. In this respect, one of Marx's great contributions was that socialism would be achieved, not by convincing the rulers, but through the struggle of the sector directly oppressed by capitalism: the working class. It is not Marx's fault that social democratic and Stalinist working-class leaders should have betrayed that struggle, halting its success, which would have led to socialism.

Now, thanks to the victory of capital, it is not only the working class that is being sacrificed by neoliberalism, but the vast majority of the global population. But still, as Derek shows, humanity is on the border of extinction because of the aggressions of capital against nature. The most affected sectors are the indigenous peoples, and to a slightly lesser extent, non-indigenous peasants (the alternative meeting to the farce in Kyoto in 1997, Vía Campesina, was an infamous example).

We should point out that the system not only attacks nature, but also, aware that the defence tool of indigenous struggle is communal and collective organisation, directs its actions to dissolving it. Indigenous people struggle collectively, sacrificing lives in the defence of Mother Earth. In defence of their own life and of the survival of the species, many indigenous activists are well aware of the latter. We must not forget that the first international meeting, 'Against Neoliberalism and for Humanity', was hosted by indigenous people in Chiapas, Mexico in 1996. It is also noteworthy that the indigenous people of Chiapas have been governing themselves in a horizontal structure for 15 years, and that their relations with urban, national and international, movements are equally horizontal.

Another characteristic of the indigenous movements of the world is what has become known as 'good living'. This idea, suggesting that living good is what is satisfactory, counters the capitalist ideology that states that money, and what you can buy with it, brings happiness, and that life should be dedicated to production and consumption. It is precisely this ideology that is increasingly quickly leading to the disappearance of the human species.

In the American hemisphere, this confrontation has been present for over five hundred years, but lately it has grown significantly with the increased aggression of capital against nature and collective organisation. This makes indigenous struggles 'ecosocialist', in European terms. In indigenous terms, they are struggles in defence of the indigenous community and of Mother Earth, who both bear different names in different languages. In my language, Quechua, it is a struggle in the defence of the 'ayllu' (community) and of 'Pachamama' (Mother Earth).

In my opinion, following Marx's logic, the most important task of the ecosocialist is to defend those at the vanguard of the struggle, the indigenous peoples and peasants in general. Of course, all sectors promoting collectivism and anti-capitalism should be supported. Many of these can be found amongst the urban population. A noteworthy example is the project, 'Sewing the Future', which starts with cotton production by Argentinean farmers, focusing next on a textiles factory taken over and administrated by its workers, continues via packing cooperatives, and culminates with the participation of the Italian consortium of fair-trade organisations, CTM Altromercato.

In this book, what Derek has made us think about is what roads of action ecosocialists should take. My opinions form a path, others will appear. Derek's concern is that talking is not enough, we must act because time is warning us; to repeat from above: *'how can we stop the train before it leaps the rails?'*

Hugo Blanco, a contemporary of Che Guevara, led a peasant revolution in Peru in 1961. A former leader of Trotsky's Fourth International (USFI), he is today a prominent ecosocialist and publishes the newspaper *Indigenous Struggle*.

1
Why Ecosocialism?

The modern economy is structurally reliant on economic growth for its stability. When growth falters – as it has done recently – politicians panic. Businesses struggle to survive. People lose their jobs and sometimes their homes. A spiral of recession looms. Questioning growth is deemed to be the act of lunatics, idealists and revolutionaries.

But question it we must. The myth of growth has failed us. It has failed the 2 billion people who still live on less than $2 a day. It has failed the fragile ecological systems we depend on for survival. It has failed spectacularly, in its own terms, to provide economic stability and secure people's livelihoods (Jackson 2009: 14).

Of course, the big problem facing all discussions of alternatives to capitalism is that there do not seem to be any alternatives. Throughout the Cold War, the alternative was state socialism or communism, but this alternative is fading fast around the globe. Asked about alternatives to capitalism today, most people draw a blank. Some would add: 'for good reason' (Speth 2008: 188).

Ecosocialism is an emerging political alternative that links socialism and ecology, arguing that ecological problems cannot be solved without challenging capitalism, and that a

1. Climate Camp, London, 2009 (Amelia Gregory)

socialism which does not respect the environment is worthless. Ecosocialism is to be found amongst green parties, social movements, socialist groups and indigenous networks. I would argue that it can be traced back to Karl Marx and lives not just in formal organizations of the left but increasingly amongst indigenous networks. Wikipedia provides a good introductory definition:

> Eco-socialism, green socialism or socialist ecology is an ideology merging aspects of Marxism, socialism, green politics, ecology and alter-globalization. Eco-socialists generally believe that the expansion of the capitalist system is the cause of social exclusion, poverty and environmental degradation through globalization and imperialism, under the supervision of repressive states and transnational structures; they advocate the dismantling of capitalism and the state, focusing on collective ownership of the means of production by freely associated producers and restoration of the commons. (<http://en.wikipedia.org/wiki/Eco-socialism>, accessed 21 February 2010)

CRISIS, WHAT CRISIS?

This book looks at why ecosocialism is necessary and how it can be encouraged to grow. This title is a call to action, not an academic text. The ecological crisis is an appropriate starting-point for the discussion. Our planet is in the grip of a severe environmental crisis and to solve it we need to construct an ecosocialist alternative. Climate change and the other ecological problems that threaten us are, above all, products of economic growth. As economies grow, the demand for oil, coal and gas to power industrial expansion is increasing and such growth tends to degrade the global environment. While it would be possible to improve living standards with less waste, our present economic system – capitalism – only works if we produce, consume and waste at ever-increasing levels. Capitalism is a system that depends on rising economic growth, so it is intrinsically linked to environmental damage. It is vital to create an alternative to capitalism that allows humanity to prosper without devastating the environment. Ecosocialism seeks to provide an alternative that is ecologically viable, socially just and meets human needs. This chapter outlines the argument for ecosocialism.

It is possible to argue that there is no environmental crisis in a fundamental or serious sense. There are many arguments that can be put forward to challenge ecosocialism. One is the notion that humanity has a long history of damaging the environment, creating horrible problems but none the less continuing to prosper. It is also true that the environment is almost constantly changing; therefore, to look for some kind of stable ecological equilibrium is likely to be misleading. Species come and go, we don't mourn the dinosaurs and the conservation of the woolly mammoth was a lost cause

10,000 years ago. The idea, implicit in some forms of green politics, of a lost Eden of pristine untainted wilderness, is a myth. The literary critic Raymond Williams argued that each generation of humanity believes that it is damaging a natural order and looks back to a previous environmental golden age; he traces examples of this approach back to Thomas More's publication of Utopia in the sixteenth century and beyond (Williams 1993: 11).

It is clear that environmental damage has occurred throughout much of human existence. Human beings have changed the environment for thousands of years and often caused severe problems as a consequence. Ancient civilisations in Iraq were destroyed partly because of salinisation: using irrigation systems for crops led to increased evaporation of water; as the water evaporated, salt was drawn to the surface of the soil. Eventually the soil was too salty to grow crops and disaster struck; one writer referred to the salt-white landscapes as a 'satanic mockery of snow' (Goudie 1981:113).

There is evidence that the madness of several Roman emperors was caused by lead pollution from their food: acidic sauces contained in tableware made from pewter, an alloy of lead, would leach lead which was then ingested by diners, contaminating their blood and brains (Wall 1994: 33). There are numerous other examples of environmental problems from the past; for example, Tobias Smollett described the rank pollution of Bath in the eighteenth century and the toxic quality of London's water supply in his novel *The Expedition of Humphry Clinker*:

If I would drink water, I must quaff the maukish contents of an open aqueduct, exposed to all manner of defilement; or swallow that which comes from the river Thames, impregnated with all the filth of London and Westminster—Human excrement is the least offensive part of the concrete, which is composed of all the drugs, minerals, and poisons, used in mechanics and manufacture, enriched with the putrefying carcases of beasts and men; and mixed with the scourings of all the wash-tubs, kennels, and common sewers, within the bills of mortality. (Smollett 1983: 114)

The fact that London's water is rather cleaner today than two centuries ago might suggest that economic growth leads, along with better regulation and the development of new technologies, to reduced pollution. Environmental problems have a long history and time and time again solutions to them have been found. However, environmental problems in the twenty-first century are increasingly global and look increasingly out of control. The most obvious and probably the most dangerous is climate change. While a minority of sceptics deny that climate change is occurring, all the indications are that rising temperatures, caused by an increase in CO_2 and other greenhouse gases, already affect us. Carbon dioxide, and other greenhouse gases such as methane and nitrous oxide, trap heat in the atmosphere, like the glass panels of a greenhouse, making the world hotter. CO_2 is released from burning fossil fuels and with the rapid increase in industrial development over the last century, huge quantities of CO_2 have been placed in the atmosphere.

This leads to increasing temperatures and increasing temperatures tend to create feedback mechanisms that further accelerate the heating of the earth. For example, as the ice caps and glaciers of the world melt, less heat is reflected from the planet's surface, because ice and snow tend to radiate heat, while dark surfaces absorb heat. Another feedback mechanism occurs as permafrost, permanently frozen marshland mainly in Siberia and Canada, melts: methane is released, which is 23 times more potent as a greenhouse gas than CO_2, that is, for every kilogram of methane released, this warms the earth 23 times as much as the equivalent kilogram of CO_2. So there is a severe risk of run-away climate change, as rising temperatures cause further rises in temperature, and so on.

Atmospheric concentrations of CO_2 and other greenhouse gases have increased from 280 parts per million (ppm) to around 430ppm in 2009 over the last century. This is the highest concentration of CO_2 in the atmosphere for over 400,000 years and if CO_2 levels continue to rise at current rates, the concentration will reach 780ppm by 2100. Methane is at its highest concentration for 650,000 years. Other greenhouse gases, such as nitrous oxide, are also rising, contributing to the increase in temperatures. Temperatures have risen by 0.7°C over the last century but are currently on course to increase by at least 3°C by 2100. Feedback mechanism could lead to far higher rises in temperature (Stern 2007).

Rising temperatures lead to rising sea levels, and will turn millions of people into refugees, as well as leading to crop failure and greater hunger. Desertification will accelerate in many parts of the world. There are a number of other major ecological consequences, one of the most worrying being acidification of the world's oceans. At present, our oceans are slightly alkaline, but they act as a carbon sink; this means much of the CO_2 produced by industrial processes is absorbed into their waters, rather than moving into the atmosphere. Carbon sinks such as the oceans and world's rainforests, which absorb CO_2, have so far reduced the greenhouse effect. However, the oceans are becoming more acidic with the absorption of CO_2, this means that it is likely that within 50 years, they will become too acidic to support calcium carbonate-shelled creatures. Many shellfish will become extinct and along with them similar species;

this will destroy the basis of food chains and is likely to devastate fish stocks. Coral reefs, which are vital to many marine ecosystems, will also be destroyed by a combination of bleaching, caused by increasing sea temperatures, and acidity, which dissolves their structures.

Climate change is just one symptom of a much wider ecological crisis. Basic biological cycles on our planet are being distorted. Rainforests are under attack, soil erosion threatens agriculture, air quality is declining and species are disappearing. Even without the threat of rising temperatures and acidification, over-fishing and pollution are wrecking the oceans. Recent reports suggest that all commercial fish stocks will be lost by 2050 (Pearce 2006). Sea-grass meadows which support marine life are declining at 7 per cent a year, putting yet another pressure on the seas, because they act as breeding grounds for many species. Dumping, industrial development and run-off from fertilisers are all causing degradation (Campbell 2009). Deforestation is accelerating, with rainforests attacked for timber, clear-cut to feed factory-farmed livestock, or assaulted to make way for oil and mineral extraction. With their loss, biodiversity falls, species become extinct and nature is fragmented.

INSANE ECONOMICS

The root of ecological crisis is economic. While cleaner technologies and better forms of environmental management have the potential to reduce environmental impact, as we consume, produce and throw more away, our impact on the environment tends to increase. After just 50 or 60 years of steady economic growth for only a small minority of the planet's inhabitants – mainly in North America, Western Europe, Australia and New Zealand – we have created a number of severe ecological problems. It is difficult to see how ever-increasing economic growth can be possible forever, for everyone on our planet.

Discovered by oceanographer Charles Moore in 1997, the plastic 'island' in the Pacific is one example of the damage that rising waste is doing to the biosphere:

> Fifty years ago, most flotsam was biodegradable. Now it is 90 per cent plastic. In 2006, the United Nations Environment Programme estimated that there were 46,000 pieces of floating plastic in every square mile of ocean. With its stubborn refusal to biodegrade, all plastic not buried in landfills – roughly half of it – sweeps into streams and sewers and then out into rivers and, finally, the ocean. Some of it – some say as much as 70 per cent – sinks to the ocean floor. The remainder floats, usually within 20 metres of the surface, and is carried into stable circular currents, or gyres 'like ocean ring-roads', says Dr Boxall. Once inside these gyres, the plastic is drawn by wind and surface currents towards the centre, where it steadily accumulates. The world's major oceans all have these gyres, and all are gathering rubbish. Although the North Pacific – bordering California, Japan and China – is the biggest, there are also increasingly prominent gyres in the South Pacific, the North and South Atlantic and the Indian Oceans. Our problems with plastics are only just beginning. (Cumming 2010)

While it is possible to blame 'greed', rising population, or the inevitable desire to have more things, economic growth is first and foremost a product of an economic system that dominates our planet: capitalism. While the definition and nature of capitalism could be discussed in some detail, it is generally agreed that capitalism is based on the pursuit of profit. Capitalism involves taking profit and reinvesting it so as to make more profit. Capitalism does not do sufficiency, there is never enough profit, it is about making more profit, which can be reinvested to make yet more profit and so on for ever. Capitalism must grow by its very nature. Firms need to reinvest; if they don't, other firms will do so and put them out of business by producing at a lower cost in the future. Capitalism is structural, whatever an individual may wish to do, if he or she runs a company, the company will ultimately go out of business if profit is not reinvested. If a firm fails to reinvest, it will be put out of business by others, because they cut costs and increase production as a result of such investment. So it is not a matter of replacing 'wicked' and uncaring people at the top with more responsible individuals.

Profit demands growth. Paradoxically, as firms become more productive by substituting machines, computers and other forms of technology for workers, economic crisis is induced. If workers are replaced with machines, consumers, who generally must work to generate income, find they have less money to spend. Also, with higher productivity, the quantity of goods produced tends to increase, which tends to push down the price. A minor intellectual industry works to investigate the varied contradictions of capitalist crisis. While those working in this industry may disagree about much, what all such theorists agree upon is the need for capitalism to expand so as to survive. Capitalism is not a conspiracy simply maintained by a small number of wicked individuals: it's a complex, embedded, global system. Growth is built into the essence of capitalism.

To keep profits flowing in, new goods must be invented and marketed. While capitalism is a highly complex system, it is clear that to survive we must produce and consume at ever-increasing rates. If we consume and produce less, the economic system we currently have moves into crisis, which is the essential reason why we have *ecological* crisis. While human beings may or may not be greedy, it is clear that we have a whole system of economics that tends to move into chaos if we become less acquisitive and spend less. Huge effort is put into sustaining and nurturing greedy behaviour to keep the profits flowing. Advertising is one way in which we are persuaded to consume more and more. In 2008, global advertising expenditure was $720 billion; despite a fall due to recession in 2009, it is growing again, particularly in India, China and other 'emerging' markets (*Hürriyet Daily News and Economic Review* 2010).

Credit is another way of sustaining consumption; in recent years, globalisation has allowed firms to increase profit by relocating to countries where wages are lower. This has transferred income on a huge scale from the poor and middle incomes to the super rich. This in turn has meant that less cash is available for consumption for the majority of the world's population. However, the availability of low-interest credit in the form of credit cards, car loans and mortgages has allowed consumption to increase.

If we spend more, this is beneficial for the current economic system and virtually everything in our society is based around getting us to produce more and consume more. If profit margins fall for a particular good, profit can be maintained by selling more of that good – even a small margin of profit adds up if it is spread over millions of items. There is a tendency to commodify new areas of life, turning activities that were free and informal into services, which are exchanged for cash, as a way of increasing economic growth. Sport is an excellent example: football is a multi-billion-pound industry with transfers of players costing millions of pounds, yet it originated as a raucous and zero-revenue competition between small villages. It's almost impossible to think of football without thinking of massive amounts of cash and a lifestyle based on conspicuous consumption. Capitalism must colonise new areas of human activity to maintain profit. Capitalism also tends to turn the natural environment into a commodity, that is, something which is controlled so it can be bought and sold. The commodification of the environment, whereby it is fenced in to make profit, tends to lead to the simplification of complex ecosystems. This in turn leads to increased environmental damage. Even a renewable energy-fuelled capitalism would still tend to degrade the environment through such commodification of nature.

In a detailed examination, Joel Kovel argues that capitalism is the 'Enemy of Nature', the efficient cause of ecological destruction. He notes:

1. Capital tends to degrade the conditions of its own production.
2. Capital must expand without end in order to exist.
3. Capital leads to a chaotic world-system increasingly polarized between rich and poor, which cannot adequately address the ecological crisis.

The combination makes an ever-growing ecological crisis an iron necessity so long as capital rules, no matter what measures are taken to tidy up one corner or another. (Kovel 2007: 38)

Defenders of the present economic system will try to find new ways of justifying the possibility of an impossible economic system based on ever-increasing resource use. Naomi Klein notes:

... the same message will return, though there may be someone new selling that message: You don't need to change. Keep consuming all you want. There's plenty more. Drill, baby, drill. Maybe there will be some technological fix that will make all our problems disappear. And that is why we need to be absolutely clear right now. Capitalism can survive this crisis. But the world can't survive another capitalist comeback. (Klein 2009)

PROSPERITY WITHOUT GROWTH

How is it possible to deal with poverty and a range of pressing needs without capitalist growth? We appear to be in a situation of choosing between capitalist growth that threatens our survival or moving to a no-growth society that will bring want to most of us. It seems we must either endorse an attitude of 'Drill, baby, drill' and assume that there will always be a new frontier or technological fix to solve our problems, or instead embrace austerity, learning to do without in a state of patched misery.

One solution to this apparent dilemma is to create a more equal society. The present economy is astonishingly unequal, with a minority enjoying an income many times higher than the average. A no-growth economy with more equal distribution would see poverty reduced for the majority. The *Economist* has noted that the median income in the US was lower in 2007 than 1978, despite nearly thirty years of continuous economic growth. Measured in 2007 currency values, the average American worker earned $45,113 in 2007, compared to $45,879 in 1978. It's astonishing, but capitalist globalisation has pushed down average wages for Americans, in real inflation-adjusted terms, despite headline growth figures (*Economist* 2009). Despite losing some of their wealth because of the recession, the world's three richest individuals – Bill Gates, Warren Buffett and Carlos Slim Helú

– were worth $112 billion in 2009, according to the Forbes list of the world's billionaires. *Forbes* recorded a total of 793 billionaires in 2009 (Whelan et al. 2009). An elite of billionaires and millionaires exists, who live largely separate lives from the rest of humanity. In July 2009, it was reported that despite the recession, planning permission was being sought for a resort hotel in Perthshire, Scotland, aimed at those with a net worth of £100 million in liquid assets. To join this club for the super-rich, a fee of £2 million a year would be required, although a modest £14,000 would buy a night's accommodation. Such excesses indicate a little redistribution would go a long way to reducing poverty (Urquhart and Watson 2009).

It is also important to realize that 'growth' within a capitalist context is a misleading guide to prosperity. Growth is not about increasing our access to the things we need or want, but simply about increasing the money value of such things. Economic growth is not measured in term of use values but exchange values. This may seem an obscure distinction but it is a vital insight if we are to overcome the ecological crisis and especially if we are to do so without reducing living standards. It may seem absurd to discuss how living standards can be improved without increasing economic growth but it is surprisingly simple. In a capitalist economy, if we buy goods and discard them and buy more, the economy grows; that is, the quantity of goods exchanged increases. However, if we could make goods that lasted longer, this would reduce growth but it would also reduce ecological impact; that is, use value would increase. There are numerous ways in which we can increase our access to the things we need with less production.

Therefore to solve the ecological crisis, which ultimately is an economic crisis, we need to develop an economy that reduces waste. This is easier than at first sight seems possible, if we contrast a capitalist economy based on increasing exchange, with an ecological economy based on use. Quite simply if we focus on use, we can increase access to goods, without accelerating the consumption, production and disposal of such goods. However, this contradicts the workings of capitalism: if we consume fewer goods because goods last longer or can be easily repaired instead of thrown away, fewer goods will be sold. If fewer goods are sold, capitalism moves into deficit. The economic system can be seen as working for a minority; I would argue that it works for the benefit of the economic system, not even primarily for an elite. After all, if we have an economic system that threatens ecological systems this damages all of humanity. Although the rich find it far easier to avoid the ecological side-effects of the current economic system, ultimately they too will be damaged by such consequences. The world's top three billionaires do not have access to a replica Earth built artificially in space to which they can escape.

Yet it is often argued that there is no workable alternative to capitalism. For example, the Soviet Union not only failed economically and socially, it was also associated with devastating environmental consequences. The Chernobyl nuclear explosion was perhaps the worst Soviet environmental disaster but pollution was widespread. By 1989, because of intensive cotton farming introduced in the 1940s, the Aral Sea had shrunk by 80 per cent:

> Much of the once-fertile land around the Sea has turned into desert and salt flats. Due to chemical pollution and erosion, the health of local people has deteriorated drastically and agricultural productivity in the region has plummeted. The birth rate is falling while infant

mortality is rising. Only 38 of the 178 animal species of the region are still extant.

In August 1988, a group of prominent Soviet scientists, writers, doctors, agricultural experts, hydrologists and geographers toured the Aral Sea region on the 'Aral-88 Expedition.' They concluded that the region is rapidly dying and will become a toxic wasteland in just a few years unless immediate action is taken to restore it. (Morris 1990)

The Soviet Union, which lacked democratic oversight, ignored local conditions and embarked on high-speed industrialisation, is rejected as an appropriate model of socialism by most on the left. Nevertheless, the idea of simply centrally planning an entire economy, even if such planning is based on democratic control, seems likely to create a number of severe problems. While some aspects of any economy, such as postal services and rail services, are likely to work more efficiently if planned centrally, central planning may lack flexibility, reduce choice and fail to protect the environment. Socialists need to rethink what they mean by collective control of the economy.

It is possible to imagine an economic system that protects the environment, creates prosperity and avoids the excesses of both capitalism and undemocratic forms of state socialism. I have argued that such an economic system can be based on the commons and forms of social sharing (Wall 2009c). Democratic planning, while necessary, is likely to be closer to a wiki than to a world parliament. The notion of a soviet, literally a council of workers and citizens that made decisions and planned production, is nearer to this notion of democratic commons, than the bureaucratic structures that came to dominate the Soviet Union.

Elinor Ostrom, a political scientist at Indiana University, was co-winner of the 2009 Nobel Prize for economics, in recognition of her work on the commons. She has spent a lifetime researching common property and found that across the globe, indigenous people and peasants have discovered ways of sharing land in ways that are ecologically sustainable and promote real prosperity (Ostrom 1990).

Former Green Party member of the New Zealand Parliament Nandor Tanczos contrasts traditional commons management with capitalist property rights:

> Our concepts of property ownership are vastly different from traditional practices of recognising use rights over various resources. A right to grow or gather food or other resources in a particular place is about meeting needs. Property ownership is about the ability to live on one side of the world and speculate on resources on the other, possibly without ever seeing it, without regard to need or consequence.
>
> The ability to 'own' property is fundamental to capitalism. Since the first limited liability companies – the Dutch and British East India Companies – were formed, we have seen the kidnapping and enslavement of 20–60 million African people and the rape, murder and exploitation of indigenous people around the world. Colonisation was primarily about mercantile empires, not political ones. It was all about forcing indigenous, communitarian people to accept private individual ownership of resources, which could then be alienated, either by being bought or stolen. (Tanczos in Wall 2005: xiv)

The commons overcomes many of the problems with traditional state socialism because it tends to be flexible and decentralised. It has an inbuilt ecological principle based on the concept of usufruct, that is, access to a resource is granted only if the resource is left in as good a form as it was when first found. By extending this concept of usufruct, we can provide the basis of an ecological economy. By providing access, the commons enables prosperity without growth; if we have access to the resources we need, we can reduce wasteful duplication.

Preserving and extending the commons for forests, seas and other ecological resources is particularly vital. In the world's rainforests, indigenous people almost universally use communal ownership to prevent ecological destruction of the forests. However, the commons principle can be applied far more widely. In the form of free software and access to the World Wide Web, it has already transformed the knowledge economy and decommodified access to culture and information. This, of course, is still imperfect: people in poorer communities may lack access to the Internet, and free Internet resources are still used to generate sales revenue. Yet it already has had an extraordinary impact and shows that alternatives to private ownership are possible. It has already redistributed income from media corporations to consumers. The legal theorist Yochai Benkler (2006) has suggested that what he terms 'social sharing' can be applied to physical goods: we use a good only some of the time, and sharing allows more access to the good, without increased production. This is already occurring with car clubs.

Roberto Verzola, an environmental activist from the Philippines has argued:

> Perfect cooperation, which leads to more abundance, is as important an economic concept as perfect competition. A properly-managed free commons, like a freely accessible public library of books, CDs and DVDs, can help create more abundance as much as an unregulated free market often leads to artificial scarcity. (Verzola 2009)

Varied forms of social sharing can massively reduce the need to produce physical goods but at the same time improve our access to them; this cuts through the contradiction between ecology and prosperity. Many people in the green movement are aware that economic growth is unsustainable, and socialists are critical of capitalism to a greater or lesser extent, but most people involved in progressive politics are unaware of the importance of the commons as a means of constructing a green and socialist economy. The commons is a solution that combines ecology with free access to resources, it does not abolish individual property but allows us to have greater use of resources with far less waste. Think of taking toys from a toy library, borrowing tools for a day, using a car pool, or even growing food on an allotment. Commons squares the circle, potentially allowing improved standards of living with far less physical impact on the environment. We need to build new commons if we are to survive and prosper as a species. Commons are almost always under assault, and globally, commons have been stolen from people and fenced off. Corporations spend billions lobbying politicians to make it difficult for individuals to access knowledge and culture for free. Corrupt academics produce 'research' arguing that commons must be destroyed.

In a practical sense, ecosocialism is a battle against enclosure. Resources for which people have cost-free access are enclosed and sold back to the individuals who originally used them for free. Such enclosure, which is based on demands for short-term profit, tends to lead to ecological destruction. Long-term conservation is ignored because in a capitalist economy once an environment has been wrecked, it is assumed that there is always a new frontier that can be crossed into new territory that can be enclosed.

An economy based on use-values that promote ecology would be based on property rights that protect the environment while providing increasing access to sustainable resources. Ecosocialism is about the battle for the commons, conserving existing commons, and extending and deepening commons. At present, most individuals are unaware of the concept of the commons, so one task for ecosocialists is to win a battle of ideas, to show that alternatives to capitalism are economically possible and ecologically vital.

Property rights are the DNA of social systems; currently, we have a system of property rights where everything is turned into a commodity for short-term gain. This system concentrates income, wealth and power in the hands of a minority. It destroys nature and it encloses and restricts human creativity. It creates an alienated humanity and threatens our very survival as a species. An alternative form of property rights based on commons has the potential to create a viable future. However, while I am sceptical of traditional socialist notions of planning, I acknowledge that planning has a role in the creation of a new ecosocialist society.

Michael Löwy, on reading the first draft of this chapter, noted:

Democratic socialist planning is not 'central', for two reasons : First) It is a planning at all levels, municipal, regional, national, continental (Europe), planetary. Second) The main decisions are not taken by any 'central' body, but by the whole concerned population, in a democratic vote ... Local transport by buses has to be locally planned. And the production of locomotives and buses has to be planned, at a national or continental level. As well as the production of electricity to produce these goods. The closing down of carbon-fueled facilities and nuclear plants has to be planned, cleaning up the monstrous waste they leave behind.

Many environmentalists have failed to criticize capitalism but capitalism is the cause of ecological destruction, so a green politics without a red analysis of capitalism will fail to develop realistic alternatives for environmental protection. Socialism while necessary is not sufficient, socialist movements in the past have amongst other failings often ignored environmental problems. There must

be a process of building ecosocialist alternatives. Socialism without
ecological concern will still wreck the planet, while ecological concern
without a socialist analysis of capitalism will fail to save it. (private
correspondence with the author)

As Dave Riley, an ecosocialist activist from Australia,
reminded me while looking at an earlier draft of this chapter,
the key problem is political not technical. Solutions are
possible but it is inadequate to simply point out that solutions,
such as the commons, permaculture and a green 'New Deal'
which would invest in renewables, exist and then expect
society to embrace them. The key is that their introduction
will involve intense political struggle. My argument is that
alternative forms of property rights that promote economic
democracy and ecological sustainability are the essential base
of a possible future, in contrast, to the impossible dream
of capitalist waste. Property rights are political in that they
determine access to resources, that is, they are about power;
but to see alternative property as a free standing solution
creates the danger of wishing for a more sophisticated fix.
To achieve solutions that work means building movements
that can win. Ecosocialist politics is the essential area that
needs to be discussed and put into action.

Creating a successful ecosocialist movement is a matter of
survival. So while this book deals with a range of theoretical
issues, it primarily aims to inspire action. My hope is that
readers will join existing ecosocialist movements or if
necessary establish them where they do not exist and work
for the change needed if future generations are to have just
that: a future. Given the accelerating ecological crisis and
the destructive nature of capitalism, practical solidarity and
focused political commitment are vital. As you read this,

thugs somewhere in the world will be physically attacking indigenous people fighting rainforest destruction. Secret meetings between corrupt local councillors and waste companies could be taking place that would result in putting an incinerator on your doorstep. Workers will be struggling against wage cuts and unemployment, they may even be raising demands for alternative green production. There will be conflict in political parties, with socialist or green organisations being forced to support rather than challenge exploitation. We need to link up and fight for a future which is ecological, just and democratic; it's absolutely crucial to get active and organized. This book aims to inspire change and to resource it.

With this aim in mind, Chapter 2 examines the real climate swindle. While climate change certainly exists and is a growing threat, there is little public awareness that the current solutions agreed at international summits are failing to reduce emissions of greenhouse gases. The current framework redistributes from poor to rich and benefits banks while doing little or nothing for the environment. The very fact that even climate change is used as a way of increasing capitalist profits is a shocking illustration of the ecosocialist case for change. Equally, unless we reduce emissions of greenhouse gases by around 90 per cent and protect carbon sinks such as the forests and oceans, the future of humanity and the rest of nature are likely to be bleak.

Chapter 3 looks at ecosocialist policies in more detail, policies aimed at tackling climate change and other ecological ills, creating social justice and real democracy. Chapter 4 outlines the evolution and origins of the ecosocialist movement from Marx and Engels to Evo Morales and John Bellamy Foster. Chapter 5 is an overview of the ecosocialist movement in Latin America where it seems currently to be making the most progress, particularly in Bolivia, Cuba, Peru and Venezuela. Chapter 6 examines ecosocialist strategies for change, asking the vital question of what is to be done? The book concludes with Chapter 7, which catalogues some of the resources available to help build an ecosocialist movement.

2
The Real Climate
Change Swindle

The Kyoto Protocol is a symbolically important expression of governments' concern about climate change. But as an instrument for achieving emissions reductions, it has failed. It has produced no demonstrable reductions in emissions or even in anticipated emissions growth ... we are witnessing that well-documented human response to failure, especially where political or emotional capital is involved, which is to insist on more of what is not working: in this case more stringent targets and timetables, involving more countries.

Prins and Rayner 2007

As individual capitalists are engaged in production and exchange for the sake of the immediate profit, only the nearest, most immediate results must first be taken into account. As long as the individual manufacturer or merchant sells a manufactured or purchased commodity with the usual coveted profit, he is satisfied and does not concern himself with what afterwards becomes of the commodity and its purchasers. The same thing applies to the natural effects of the same actions ... In relation to nature, as to society, the present mode of production is predominantly concerned only about the immediate, the most tangible result.

Engels 1987: 463–4

2. Climate Camp, London, 2009 (Amelia Gregory)

Climate change is perhaps the most significant threat to the global environment; however, effective action to deal with it still seems a distant prospect, despite the urgency needed. This is partly because the need to reduce fossil fuel use threatens important vested interests from car manufacture to oil and coal extraction. Because of this a well-funded industry of denial has emerged. In the 1950s, '60s and '70s, cigarette manufacturers pumped money into research aimed at showing that smoking was safe. Such well-funded scepticism slowed the introduction of measures to reduce smoking and as a direct result millions of unnecessary deaths occurred. Today there is a similar campaign to suggest that climate change is not occurring, or if it is occurring, it is not caused by the burning of fossil fuels. As evidence mounts that they are wrong, the sceptics are variously arguing that it is too late to stop climate change or that rising temperatures are beneficial. Their arguments are varied, and often contradictory, but any argument to shift concern away from carbon-extracting industries will apparently do.

Between 1998 and 2005, Exxon Mobile gave $16 million to fund advocacy organisations, ranging from well-known right-wing think tanks such as the Cato Institute and the Heritage Foundation to groups like the Centre for the Study of Carbon Dioxide and Global Change, whose titles suggested they were neutral scientific bodies (Reitman 2007). Yet the Centre for the Study of Carbon Dioxide and Global Change is headed by a director who has worked for Peabody, the giant US coal company, as an environmental adviser. The Centre argues that climate change is a positive process and that increased carbon dioxide will bring many benefits, such as increased plant growth.

Clearly the sceptics are wrong and the risk, as we have noted, is that feedback mechanisms could make climate change far worse than initially predicted. The sceptics have been challenged by virtually the entire scientific community. However, what has been forgotten in the ongoing battle between the sceptics and mainstream science is that there is another climate change swindle which is tragic yet largely ignored; that is, the swindle that has substituted practical action to deal with climate change with a system that is ineffective. The current international framework to deal with climate change, at conferences such as Kyoto and Copenhagen, does not work. Huge efforts are being put into solutions which have failed. Despite all the talk and meetings and media coverage that daily show the severity of the problem, emissions of CO_2 and other greenhouse gases keep rising. But like any good 'con', the system makes a lot of money for those who really understand how it works.

The global approach, known as 'cap and trade', which aims to gain the approval and active cooperation of every country in the world, is based on a system of carbon trading. The idea is simple: carbon dioxide and other emissions will be limited in every part of the world – this is the idea of the 'cap'. This in principle appears to be a reasonable way of tackling climate change. Each country in the world will be set a fixed quantity of emissions it must not exceed. If the limits are tight enough, emissions will fall, slowing and perhaps eventually stopping the rise in global temperatures. The 'trade' part of 'cap and trade' means that countries that reduce their emissions enough will be able to sell the right to produce CO_2 and other greenhouse gases to other countries, which have made greater cuts. This system should, in principle, provide an important financial incentive to reduce emissions. Clearly however, there is a problem if a system aimed at reducing emissions to tackle climate change, especially one which, rather than being a theoretical or local scheme, aims to involve every country in the world, does not work. While we hear a great deal from climate deniers arguing that climate change is nothing to worry about, there is far less debate about the flawed nature of the current system aimed at tackling it.

Understanding the climate change swindle, the real one, not the supposed conspiracy by weather forecasters to increase their overtime pay, is vitally important. It is important because climate change is such a significant threat to all of us on planet Earth. It is also a good illustration of the power of a global capitalist economy; even the damage produced to the environment by capitalist growth is used to find ways of financing more profit-orientated expansion. The current system of dealing with climate change is accepted by the great and the good because, while it is ineffective and as we shall see even counter-productive at reducing emissions, it does make money for banks in particular and corporations in general. To have a positive effect on climate change, the current framework must be replaced by policies that reduce emissions. An 'Emperor's no clothes' syndrome exists for most environmentalists. Many environmentalists refuse to criticise the current framework, because until recently countries with climate change-denying leaders like George Bush's United States or former Prime Minister Howard's Australia refused to participate in *any* system to reduce greenhouse gases. The argument goes that the current system is better than nothing, yet in some ways it may have, as we shall see, a negative effect, accelerating rather than slowing climate change. Even if it was not on balance negative, given the potentially dreadful consequences of climate change, merely 'better than nothing' is not good enough.

CLIMATE CHAOS CASH

It is often argued that given the global nature of environmental problems such as climate change, world-wide rather than merely local solutions are necessary. However, the global framework of conferences, UN institutions and committees is firmly controlled not by scientists or even elected officials but by corporate interests. They have made sure that notions such as 'sustainable development' work to sustain profits rather than to protect the environment. The notion of economic growth as a way of reducing poverty is the official justification, but the desire to accumulate profit dominates international environmental policy making, in the same way that it dominates global sport, global entertainment or global medicine. Environmental concern and poverty reduction are labels attached to items bought and sold for the benefit of a business elite locked into a logic of profit seeking. Attempts to go beyond such logic are ignored by the powerful interests that shape global climate policy.

The problem of climate change has been widely recognized since the late 1980s and attempts to tackle it began at the Rio Earth Summit in 1992. The Rio conference produced the Agenda 21 document, which outlined plans for environmental protection for the twenty-first century. The document suggested that adapting the market can solve environmental problems, using market-based instruments to provide incentives for change. Such a market-based approach, rather than regulation aimed at restricting the production of greenhouse gases, dominates the official response to climate change at present.

John Bellamy Foster argues that corporate lobbyists shaped this policy framework, noting the influence of the Business Council for Sustainable Development, a body whose members included 'Chevron Oil, Volkswagen, Mitsubishi, Nissan, Nippon Steel, S.C. Johnson and Son, Dow Chemical, Browning-Ferris Industries, ALCOA, Dupont, Royal/Dutch Shell' and other businesses involved in oil extraction, car manufacture, aluminium smelting, etc. (2009: 133). Foster argues that the second Earth Summit held in Johannesburg in 2002 continued this process of constructing pro-business environmentalism. The pro-business environmental approach suggests there is no intrinsic conflict between business and the environment, because 'natural capitalism' allows firms to grow while reducing their environmental impact through efficiency gains.

According to its advocates, *natural capitalism* 'describes a future in which business and environmental interests increasingly overlap, and in which businesses can better satisfy their customers' needs, increase profits, and help solve environmental problems all at the same time' (Holender 2006: 160).

There have been numerous reports, meetings and official events that have reinforced this approach. While some business interests have been keen to argue that climate change can be safely ignored, major polluting firms have been seeking to find ways of dealing with climate change while maintaining or enhancing profit. In 2005, the G8 Climate Change Roundtable, which included BP, British Airways, HSBC, Petrobras, Rio Tinto, Toyota and Volkswagen, argued that 'Policy frameworks that use market-based mechanisms to set clear, transparent and consistent price signals over the long term offer the best hope for unleashing needed innovation and competition' (World Economic Forum 2005). The influence of environmental NGOs over climate policy has been marginal compared to that of many of the world's largest and most polluting corporate bodies. In addition, many environmental NGOs are actually funded by corporate polluters and banks; for example, the HSBC bank which invests in tar sand oil production, donates to the World Wide Fund for Nature (Carrell 2002).

In 2006, Professor Nicholas Stern released the *Stern Review on the Economics of Climate Change*, commissioned by the British government. The report argued that climate change is a severe problem that must be faced by reducing climate change gases and will create major human and financial costs if allowed to continue. Stern, a former vice-chair of the World Bank, unsurprisingly advocated the market-based approach, arguing that climate change is a product of market failure which gives rise to external costs. The solution to what Stern described as the greatest market failure in history was to adapt the market using cap and trade along with a possible carbon tax (Stern 2007). It's instructive that an economist rather than an environmental scientist wrote the British government's most important document on climate change policy. While the description of the ill effects of climate change put forward by Stern are sobering, it is also true that he was chosen as a figure who could provide a business-friendly market-based solution to carbon change.

Stern noted that climate change could lead to the physical destruction of the world's most important financial centres through the flooding of cities like London and New York due to rising sea levels. Tackling climate change would be far wiser financially than letting it occur. He is also enthusiastic about carbon trading because it will create a huge amount of business for bankers. This is already occurring and of course, London as one of the world's main financial centres is gaining from the process.

This market-based approach was already enshrined in the Kyoto Protocol, part of the UN's framework for dealing with climate change, and introduced in December 1997. It provides an international legal agreement to limit CO_2, methane, nitrous oxide and other gases, which cause climate change.

Over 180 countries have signed the protocol and agreed to reduce emissions. It is based on emissions trading; as we noted earlier, countries that cannot reduce their emissions can buy permits to pollute from countries that produce less CO_2 and other greenhouse gases than they have agreed. It also includes the Clean Development Mechanism, a process whereby businesses can buy the right to continue polluting by funding projects aimed at reducing greenhouse gases in the south of the globe.

The system is similar to carbon offset, where consumers who produce greenhouse gases can pay for someone else to reduce their impact on the environment to compensate. Carbon offset is a voluntary scheme, which has been encouraged by airline companies, 'environmental' entrepreneurs and those who like to fly but feel bad about the consequences of a jet-set lifestyle. Carbon offset is used to offset not just emissions but guilt; those who take, for example, a transatlantic flight, generating huge amounts of CO_2 from each trip, can spend money with a carbon offset, so as to feel better. Typically, the carbon offset fee will pay for tree planting or other schemes that are said to reduce or absorb emissions. However, carbon offset is rarely effective. If we take tree planting, it is clear that trees will only slowly absorb CO_2 and if cut down will emit it again; it is far better to prevent the erosion of rainforests and other environments that absorb carbon. In addition, the tree planting may not involve native species and can lead to local people being pushed off their land.

Such problems are well illustrated by the first carbon offset project in the world. A new 183-megawatt coal-fired power plant in Connecticut was allowed to go ahead in 1989, because of a 'mitigation' project in the Western Highlands region of Guatemala:

The project entailed planting 50 million non-native pine and eucalyptus trees on some 40,000 small farm holdings in this deeply impoverished region ... An external evaluation revealed that subsistence activities undertaken by the largely indigenous population, such as gathering fuelwood for cooking, were now criminalized and conflicts erupted over rights to the trees, exacerbating existing tensions over access to resources and local decision-making. Initially the tree species used were largely inappropriate for the area and resulted in land degradation. The evaluators, Winrock International, concluded in 1999 – 10 years after the project began – that AES's offset target was falling far below the expected level. By 2001, farmers were still not receiving direct payments for the trees they planted and looked after and many were not aware that these trees were being used for storing carbon for AES. (Ma'anit 2006)

Matters have not improved since this first scheme in 1989. The *Financial Times* found, in April 2007, widespread abuse of carbon offset which included many examples of people and organizations buying worthless credits that do not yield any reductions in carbon emissions or gaining carbon credits on the basis of efficiency gains from which they have already benefited substantially.

DuPont, the chemicals company, invites consumers to pay $4 to eliminate a tonne of carbon dioxide from its plant in Kentucky that produces a potent greenhouse gas called HFC-23. But the equipment required to reduce such gases is relatively cheap. DuPont refused to comment and declined to specify its earnings from the project, saying it was at too early a stage to discuss. (Harvey and Fidler 2007)

While carbon offset has become big business – $62 billion in 2010 according to the *Financial Times* – it is not part of the official framework; however, emissions trading works in much the same way. Both carbon offset and the international emissions trading system, even if they were effective at reducing greenhouse gas production, allow those who are relatively well-off to continue polluting by buying credits from those who are poorer. In practice, however, emissions trading has also failed, like carbon offset, to limit emissions. Emissions trading is most advanced in the European Union, where a fully developed trading system has been running for a number of years.

The European Union's Emissions Trading System, which paves the way for full participation in the Kyoto Protocol, has allowed firms to increase their greenhouse gas emissions. In its first phase, carbon permits were given away rather than sold and allowed firms to produce more CO_2 than they had previously produced. In the second phase, which started in 2008, firms were expected to make £4.6 billion from selling permits, not because they became more efficient or shifted to renewable energy, but because the permits were again too generous (Peter 2009).

This seems to be a rather pointless exercise, you might think, but a huge carbon market has evolved. The process of carbon trading, according to Larry Lohmann of The Corner House, a research group based in Britain, is similar to the banking practices that led to the 2008 bank collapses and financial crisis (Lohmann 2009). The Kyoto Protocol has put bankers in charge of tackling climate change, after they have failed the economy. Systems of 'hedging' that are supposed to reduce risk tend to evolve into sophisticated forms of gambling.

SHORT-SELLING THE FUTURE

Carbon 'hedging' is now taking place, as well as even more esoteric forms of financial manipulation. Short-selling, which is a highly controversial way of making cash, by betting on company failure, has even become part of the financial strategy of 'green' hedge funds. That is, if 'green' companies go bankrupt, the 'green' hedge fund can make money when they fail. As Richard Bookbinder, who launched TerraVerde Capital Partners LLC, noted: 'Short-selling opportunities will exist because many of these green companies are not going to make it, and that's why the opportunity to make money in this space is greater in a hedge fund format than it is in a long-only format ... We think we're going to find a real benefit by investing in these strategies' (Benjamin 2009).

The value of this carbon market rose to $126 billion in 2008, according to the World Bank, a twelvefold rise from 2005:

> A total 4.8 billion tons of carbon dioxide, the main greenhouse gas blamed for global warming, were traded last year, up 61 percent from the 3 billion traded in 2007.
>
> The value of the European Union's Emissions Trading Scheme, the 27-nation bloc's flagship weapon in its fight against climate change, rose by 87 percent to $92 billion last year, the bank said.
>
> That scheme traded 3.1 billion tons of emissions permits last year, up from 2.1 billion in 2007.
>
> The rest of the market was made up mostly by secondary trade in Kyoto Protocol carbon offsets, which companies buy to cover their own emissions or sell to make profit. (Chestney and Szabo 2009)

Greenhouse gases continued to rise between 2005 and 2008; although the rate of increase slowed, a slowdown due to rising oil prices rather than carbon credits seems to have been the cause.

There are even fears of a sub-prime carbon market, with companies selling dubious financial products, analogous to the sub-prime mortgage market, where risky mortgages were repackaged with other debts and sold on, creating bank collapses and financial chaos. Climate change is being used to fuel speculative finance with scams making billions, but doing nothing to protect the planet.

Part of the system at a global level involves, like carbon offset, the process of polluting industries buying the right to continue polluting by funding projects for greenhouse gas reduction in the south of the globe. This is known as the Clean Development Mechanism (CDM) and involves paying polluters in the south of the globe to clean up their production. One imagines this would mainly involve funding new sources of renewable energy production or the introduction of new cleaner technologies. In practice, it often involves paying polluting companies for efficiency investments they would have made without the CDM. Even if this was seen as desirable, there are a huge number of loopholes that can be exploited by firms to milk the system, and there is evidence of thinly disguised fraud. For all these reasons, hypothetical reductions in greenhouse gases rarely occur and the CDM can be used to expand production, which creates more damage to the environment. For example:

India's Tata Power is building one of the world's largest coal-fired plants in Gujarat, which, when it becomes operational, will pump out 23.4 million tonnes of carbon dioxide (CO_2) a year. The International Finance Corporation, which is helping to finance the plant, claims that it will emit 3.6 million tonnes less of CO_2 each year than any other subcritical coal plant in India.

If it was able to sell those reductions at current market prices, it could earn around 70 million euros per year. In the 2007/2008 financial year, Tata Power's net profits were up 25%, reaching US$184 million. (Smith 2008)

Tata has an appalling environmental record; for example, in West Bengal, farmers committed suicide after the company seized their land to build a car plant. At its steel works in Orissa, protesters objecting to pollution were shot. It seems odd that a CDM is used to fund coal-fired power stations: 'Carbon finance being used to subsidize the fossil fuel industry is possibly the illogical logical conclusion of the carbon market. The construction of such new coal-dependent energy infrastructure is locking us into decades more of massive greenhouse gas emissions' (ibid.).

The social ecologist Brian Toker has argued that CDMs

> ... are subsidizing the already routine destruction of byproducts from China's rising production of ozone-destroying hydrofluorocarbons, minor retooling of highly polluting pig iron smelters in India, and methane capture from a notoriously toxic landfill in South Africa. One of the most notorious cases is that of the French chemical company, Rhodia, which is anticipating a billion dollars in offset credits in exchange for a $15 million investment in 1970s-vintage technology to destroy the potent greenhouse gas nitrous oxide in its facility in South Korea. (Tokar 2009)

A German study of UN-approved carbon offset projects in 2007 reported that as much as 86 per cent of offset-funded projects would have been carried out anyway (ibid.). In turn, Reduced Emissions from Deforestation and Forest Degradation (REDD)s are part of the system aimed at giving financial rewards to countries that maintain their forests. The REDD approach is still being designed, but its basic approach is to pay for forest conservation. However, this looks likely to translate into the commodification of land owned by indigenous people and peasants who maintain forests generally far better than corporations which seek to exploit forests for financial gain. There are some fears that REDD will be used to fund monocultures of fast-growing trees like eucalyptus, which replace biodiverse rainforests. The idea of leaving indigenous people to manage rainforests has not apparently occurred to the policy makers.

BIOFUELS KILL

Another approach to climate change policy has been the promotion of biofuels. At first glance, biofuels appear environmentally attractive. What could be more eco-friendly than growing crops to fuel cars and other motor vehicles? However, biofuels create even more climate damage than fossil fuels. Biofuels are grown, which requires energy, generally from fossil fuels; non-organic agriculture uses fertilisers and pesticides that are derived from fossil fuels as well, and so a tank of biofuel still relies on CO_2 production. The most popular biofuel crop, palm oil, is grown in tropical regions of the world in countries such as Colombia, Indonesia and Malaysia; it is often obtained by cutting down rainforests and replacing them with palm oil plantations. Such biofuels devastate the environment and accelerate climate change by wrecking carbon sinks in the form of existing forests. They often also reduce the land available for food crops: in the US, farmers are growing maize to fuel cars, which has reduced the supply of edible maize leading to increased maize prices in Mexico and much of Central America.

Biofuels are strongly promoted as a solution to dwindling oil reserves and climate change. President Obama is strongly promoting biofuels, as is the European Union. One EU Directive states that 5.75 per cent of vehicle fuel in the

EU must come from biofuels. The biggest single source of biofuels for the EU and a major source for the US is Colombia. However, much of the land used to grow biofuels in Colombia has been taken from local people by right-wing paramilitaries. So EU and US attempts to boost biofuels not only damage the environment but also are closely linked to human rights abuse. According to Dominic Nutt, a British researcher from Christian Aid:

> The paramilitaries are not subtle when it comes to taking land … They simply visit a community and tell landowners, 'If you don't sell to us, we will negotiate with your widow.'
>
> Milvia Dias's father was executed by paramilitaries to gain land for palm oil.
>
> A search party found him with his throat cut and seven stab wounds in his torso.
>
> 'We held the funeral at 5pm the same day and we ran away the next morning,' said Dias. The land is now covered in palm trees owned by Urapalma, a Colombian enterprise that has repeatedly been accused in court proceedings of improperly invading private property.
>
> Nutt said last week that he had heard stories of paramilitaries cutting off the arms of illiterate peasants and applying their fingerprints to land sale documents. In many cases, Nutt added, the land is collectively owned by indigenous people or Afro-Colombians and protected by federal laws that courts seem unable or unwilling to enforce. (Allen-Mills 2007)

The Afro-Colombians, communities who live an ecological lifestyle, are descended from African slaves brought to Latin America, and are especially threatened by EU demands for biofuels. Tens of thousands of Afro-Colombians have been forced to live in shanty towns in Colombian cities such as Bogotá, their land having been taken for plantations to produce 'green' fuel for cars in Paris, London and Brussels.

In Indonesia, indigenous people are similarly threatened by the expansion of biofuels, while in African states, the forests are being logged to create plantations to run vehicles.

The aim of biofuels, as always, is to keep business as usual moving ahead, irrespective of environmental or social cost. The major industrialists don't want us to buy fewer cars or to fly less, so 'solutions' to climate change are fine unless they involve us spending less on polluting commodities. Driving and flying must continue unchecked; flying less or using the bus are not preferred options for capitalism. Everything is made into a market solution. Those who get in the way tend to be sacrificed – the Afro-Colombians, for example, are expendable. Markets are presented as common-sense, flexible solutions, but the approach of pricing everything on the planet and making it available for sale, involves the acceleration of inequality. The wealthy can buy the right to pollute more and the poor pick up the bill, in the case of biofuels, even at gunpoint.

Biofuels and carbon trading are accompanied by an individualistic approach to climate change. The burden is shifted from governments and corporations on to individuals who are urged to change their habits. While leading a green lifestyle is worthwhile, the current approach, which stresses personal action rather than more fundamental social and economic change, is problematic. Most emissions, perhaps surprisingly, are not produced by individual consumers, so lifestyle change, even if very radical, will have a limited effect on its own. Derrick Jensen notes that Al Gore's film *An Inconvenient Truth*:

> ... helped raise consciousness about global warming. But did you notice that all of the solutions presented had to do with personal

consumption—changing light bulbs, inflating tires, driving half as much—and had nothing to do with shifting power away from corporations, or stopping the growth economy that is destroying the planet? Even if every person in the United States did everything the movie suggested, U.S. carbon emissions would fall by only 22 percent. Scientific consensus is that emissions must be reduced by at least 75 percent worldwide. (Jensen 2009)

Lifestyle change is often linked to corporate projects designed to make the companies who produce the most greenhouse gases look environmentally friendly. The energy generator EDF spent millions of pounds promoting a 'Green Day' on 10 July 2009 in the UK, aimed at encouraging community projects to reduce CO_2. The day gave the appearance that EDF was a green company committed to reducing CO_2 emissions. Yet 49 per cent of EDF's power comes from coal, 12 per cent from nuclear and just 6 per cent from renewables. The firm is pressing ahead with a new generation of coal and nuclear power plants but its marketing seems to suggest that it makes the environment its priority. Marketing projects to make polluters look green are often more attractive to companies than making actual changes that promote ecology. For decades, oil companies have funded tree planting, 'green days' and environmental NGOs as a distraction from their anti-environmental actions.

BEYOND PETROLEUM?

British Petroleum launched a marketing campaign using the slogan 'Beyond Petroleum', yet there is little indication that the company is moving beyond oil production and has recently invested heavily to produce oil from the highly polluting tar sands of Alberta in Canada. The environmental journalist Fred Pearce is sceptical of BP's claims:

> Let's get real. BP likes to say that it is investing $1.5bn (£980,000) a year in 'alternative' energy. True, I am sure. But that word 'alternative' is clever. Delve a little further and it turns out that BP's alternative energy division includes not just wind and solar and biofuels but also natural gas-fired power stations. Natural gas may be less polluting than coal and oil, but at the end of the day it's a fossil fuel filling the atmosphere with CO_2. Alternative? Not by my definition.
>
> Also sheltering in the alternative energy division is BP's 'emissions assets business', which makes money out of carbon trading, and a venture capital unit. But even if we lump all this 'alternative' activity together, it still only makes up 7% of the company's planned $21bn (£13.85bn) investment this year. The remaining 93% is oil, spiced up with some coal. (Pearce 2008)

It is instructive to contrast the amounts of money spent by firms advertising their environmental virtues compared with their audited spending on renewable energy or other real environmental improvements. Environmental concern is bought and sold by large firms, just like any other commodity.

The major causes of greenhouse gas emissions are largely ignored by the global efforts aimed at reducing greenhouse gas emissions. Coal is a good example. Coal is the biggest single source of CO_2, yet coal production is profitable, so there are few calls from politicians and business leaders to produce less coal. In Britain, new coal-fired power stations are planned and it is hoped that a new technology will emerge to remove the CO_2 from coal. The simpler solution of producing energy from clean sources is unpalatable to the powers that be. At present, carbon capture and storage is untested and if as little as 1 per cent of the CO_2 stored was to escape each year, it would have little effect on reducing climate change.

Air travel is one of the fastest growing sources of greenhouses gases, but there were no clauses in the Kyoto Protocol which called for the reduction of flights or to slow the pace of airport construction. Until recently, air travel had not even been included in the emissions trading system, although airlines now see it as a way of continuing to expand flights. British Airways, for example, argues that offsetting can be used to make flights carbon neutral and 'believe that carbon trading is by far the best mechanism for limiting aviation's impact on climate change while allowing the industry to grow' (<www.enviro.aero> (n.d.)).

Although there is much noise, media coverage and contributions from the great and the good – from CEOs to globe-trotting celebrities – the global framework for dealing with climate change has failed. Solutions that involve challenging business interests are unacceptable, because in a world dominated by the market, business interests are in charge. Everywhere, the criteria for climate policy is based on potential impact on profit rather than effectiveness in preventing catastrophe. Cuts in fossil fuel production would be problematic for oil companies, so we have the bizarre spectacle of a media blizzard of news about climate change and politicians insisting they are taking action, combined with a mad scramble to extract as much oil as possible as quickly as possible. The current system could be reformed; for example, secondary trading in complex carbon instruments could be outlawed, emission permits could be tightened to cut potential emissions, and attempts made to stamp on carbon fraud. However, even with these changes, the system would be full of flaws, as climate justice researcher Kevin Smith has noted: 'Such schemes allow us to sidestep the most fundamentally effective response to climate change that we can take, which is to leave fossil fuels in the ground. This is by no means an easy proposition for our heavily fossil fuel dependent society; however, we all know it is precisely what is needed' (Smith 2006).

There are battles raging across every continent of the world to stop oil and coal extraction. Indigenous people are often at the centre of these struggles, concerned that extraction will damage the health of local people and wreck their environment, while cash flows to distant shareholders. Indigenous people also work hard to protect the rainforests and other carbon sinks vital for the conservation of the global environment. Rather than the failed policy of emissions trading, action on climate change should start with these struggles around land rights and preservation. Rather than putting bankers in charge of climate change, it would be better to give indigenous people a major say in decision making; however, they have been excluded from international climate conferences. In December 2007, indigenous people from Asia, Africa and Latin America demonstrated outside the Bali Climate Conference in Indonesia:

Surrounded by demonstrators wearing paper gags reading UNFCCC (United Nations Framework Convention on Climate Change), Marcial Arias, one of Panama's Kuna people, made a passionate plea for the world to listen. 'There are no name places for indigenous people, there are no seats for indigenous people,' said Arias, referring to a UN conference in Bali, Indonesia on future plans for fighting climate change. 'They want us to beg on our knees to be given the floor, but we have the right to participate,' he said. (Innovation 2007)

Another important element of an effective strategy to deal with climate change is a green industrial revolution, based on changing structures so we can live better with less energy.

We need structural changes so that we can live well without emitting as many greenhouse gases. The market won't change the structure, and pricing policies, even if properly developed and implemented, are inadequate. Members of the Climate Camp have made this point particularly clearly:

> Setting a price for carbon isn't even a very good way of stopping people emitting it. We use fossil fuels because we started using them and then it became a habit, this is called lock-in – the way a technology becomes ingrained in society even though it isn't the best available – a good example is the QWERTY keyboard – this arrangement of letters was designed because typewriters jam if you type too fast, on computers this isn't a problem but we still use the same technology that is obviously less good, and even if other keyboards were cheaper people wouldn't use them. (Climate Camp 09 2009)

NEW GREEN POWER

Generating clean energy is vital in combating climate change. In Britain, Green Party leader and Member of Parliament Caroline Lucas has been calling for a green 'New Deal' that would see major investment in clean energy (see <http://www. greennewdealgroup.org>).

Investment in trains, buses and other forms of public transport is necessary if people are to reduce car use; likewise, planning laws need to encourage local production and local facilities such as schools and hospitals, so as to make carbon reduction easier. These structural changes would make it easier for individuals to reduce their contribution to climate change. If shops are local and services are local, a reduction in car use is practical. One of the few countries to have introduced such policies is Cuba, a country that has promoted public transport, investment in renewables and has created low-emissions-based permaculture to supplement agricultural production. During the 1990s, when the collapse of the Soviet Union meant the end of cheap oil imports, Cuba urgently needed to move to an economy less reliant on fossil fuels. The World Wide Fund for Nature recognised Cuba as the only country in the world to achieve sustainable development, so as to increase human development without imposing an unsustainable pattern of consumption. The example of Cuba is a good indication of what can be done to tackle climate change while raising human development. Cuba has not used carbon trading – instead it has sought to cut carbon. It's simple when you think about it.

Peace is good for the planet: war is a source of human misery and with it, rising emissions. The military in countries like the US and Britain is a vast generator of pollution. The US military is the country's single largest user of fossil fuels, as the US is currently at war in Iraq and Afghanistan and has military bases in over 150 countries. According to the *New York Times*, 20 July, 2009, 'In 2006 alone, the Pentagon bought 110 million barrels of oil and 3.8 billion kilowatts of electricity. To put that in perspective, it's about what the entire world uses each day' (Leber 2009). US military might is deployed to try to maintain oil supplies from the Middle East. It is instructive to examine how much emphasis is placed on individual consumer energy demand, compared to the huge consumption of fossil fuels by the armies of the world. A massive reduction in the military would reduce emissions.

Factory farming is another a source of climate change, one that must be challenged but is generally ignored. A research report from the FAO found that 18 per cent of all climate change emissions are from livestock production, which is a bigger share than that from transport. Accounting for 9 per cent of anthropogenic carbon dioxide emissions, livestock production generates 'even bigger shares of emissions of other gases with greater potential to warm the atmosphere: as much as 37 percent of anthropogenic methane', mostly from cows and sheep, 'and 65 percent of anthropogenic nitrous oxide, mostly from manure' (FAO 2006).

We need to move to a world where we eat less meat, that farms the meat it produces in a sustainable way and uses any waste produced to generate energy rather than to emit climate-changing methane. There is a strong argument for promoting vegetarianism as an ecological alternative, while recognising that indigenous and other traditional diets are sustainable, unlike factory farming.

Most fundamentally we need an ecosocialist economy where prosperity without waste becomes the goal of society. The assumption that we can maintain infinite economic growth with increasing production and consumption forever is madness. The present economy is based on bulimia and obesity. 'Enough' must replace 'more'. A healthier and socially just alternative is necessary to global capitalism. Bolivian President Evo Morales has argued: 'Climate change is not the product of human beings in general, but rather the on-going capitalist system, based on unlimited industrial development. We must do away with the exploitation of human beings and with the pillage of our natural resources. The north needs to pay the ecological debt, rather than the countries paying the external debt' (Morales 2009: 143).

The current system that even makes bets on the destruction of the global environment, as a way of cashing in on catastrophe, must be replaced.

Much environmental concern fails to deal with the fundamental issues of power both political and economic. Rob Newman, a British writer and comedian, notes that discussions of climate change fail to debate the issue of political power. At present, the powerful bend environmental policy making to serve their short-term needs:

> Much discussion of energy, with never a word about power, leads to the fallacy of a low-impact, green capitalism somehow put at the service of environmentalism. In reality, power concentrates around wealth. Private ownership of trade and industry means that the decisive political force in the world is private power. The corporation will outflank every puny law and regulation that seeks to constrain its profitability. It therefore stands in the way of the functioning democracy needed to tackle climate change. Only by breaking up corporate power and bringing it under social control will we be able to overcome the global environmental crisis. (Newman 2006)

While there is some awareness of the threat of climate change, necessary action is largely avoided. Real solutions to climate change, great and small, are ignored. We live in a world where climate change 'action' is made compatible with more cars, more flights, increased coal and oil extraction and, above all, greater profit. The current framework rewards polluting companies, hedge funds and banks. Despite the urgent need to reduce emissions, the accumulation of capital remains more important than the preservation of the global environment. Former director of the Sierra Club and leader of the Canadian Green Party Elizabeth May has argued, 'The reality is that Kyoto is the only legally binding agreement to reduce greenhouse gases. When you're drowning and someone throws you a lifeboat, you can't wait for another one to come along' (Athanasiu 2005).

However, the global framework is no lifeboat, it's more like a large stone: if we pick it up, we will more likely sink than reach the safety of the shore. The urgent need for climate change solutions that work is perhaps the strongest argument possible for political action which challenges the corporate interests that generate greenhouse gases. To prevent climate catastrophe, an ecosocialist alternative is necessary and urgent.

3
An Ecosocialist Manifesto

Socialism, Communism, or whatever one chooses to call it, by converting private property into public wealth, and substituting co-operation for competition, will restore society to its proper condition of a thoroughly healthy organism, and insure the material wellbeing of each member of the community. It will, in fact, give Life its proper basis and its proper environment.

Wilde 1971: 4

Our problem is how to craft rules at multiple levels that enable humans to adapt, learn, and change over time so that we are sustaining the very valuable natural resources that we inherited so that we may be able to pass them on. I am deeply indebted to the indigenous peoples in the U.S. who had an image of seven generations being the appropriate time to think about the future. I think we should all reinstate in our mind the seven-generation rule. When we make really major decisions, we should ask not only what will it do for me today, but what will it do for my children, my children's children, and their children's children into the future.

Ostrom 2008

3. Australian Green Party and Socialist Alliance activists (Peter Campbell)

This chapter explores ecosocialist policies – it is a little like a mini-manifesto or a first-cut utopia. However, there are a number of problems in outlining an ecosocialist vision for a society based on ecosocialist policies. For a start, there is some danger of simply repeating green and socialist policies found elsewhere, and there is certainly an overlap between the policies of green parties on, say, waste reduction and agriculture and an ecosocialist approach. Likewise, traditional socialist demands for wealth redistribution and trade union rights are uncontroversial from an ecosocialist point of view, and these demands are also embraced by the majority of Greens. There are, however, vital distinctions that must be made between ecosocialism and much traditional ecological and socialist policy making. For example, socialists have usually advocated large-scale industrial expansion and failed to examine the potential costs of destructive development, while Greens have sometimes embraced flawed market-based solutions such as carbon trading.

Equally detailed policy prescriptions can be a substitute for political action; we could spend time painting a picture of utopia, rather than thinking strategically about how we get to a better world. Policy making can sometimes distract from the task of changing society. In a capitalist society where virtually everything marches to the drumbeat of profit accumulation, it is difficult to think outside of the social reality within which we are enclosed. Every time we construct possible alternatives there is a danger that we reproduce unconsciously the norms of our present society. Neither is ecosocialism something that can be proclaimed by a set of experts and imposed on humanity. One person's perfect society may be another individual's well-built prison; the future must be based on democratic choices:

Reflecting the need for democratic solutions that draw upon participation, given the complexity of ecological systems, Elinor Ostrom, the Nobel Prize-winning economist who studied the commons, noted:

We need to be aware that overly simplistic policy responses to the diversity of problems facing us can frequently make things worse rather than better. Reliance on panaceas is itself a major environmental problem! No single cure-all is sufficient to solve the complex, multi-level, interactive problems that constitute the human environment. (Ostrom 2006)

For similar reasons, the authors of *Whose Common Future* argued:

It is customary to conclude a paper such as this with policy rec-ommendations ... A space for the commons cannot be created by

> economists, development planners, legislators, 'empowerment' specialists or other paternalistic outsiders. To place the future in the hands of such individuals would be to maintain the webs of power that are currently stifling commons regimes. One cannot legislate the commons into existence; nor can the commons be reclaimed simply by adopting 'green techniques' such as organic agriculture, alternative energy strategies or better public transport – necessary and desirable though such techniques often are. Rather, commons regimes emerge through ordinary people's day-to-day resistance to enclosure, and through their efforts to regain livelihoods and the mutual support, responsibility and trust that sustain the commons. (Hildyard et al. 1995)

None the less, despite such difficulties, it is important to outline an ecosocialist vision both to inspire support for ecosocialism and to aid the development of practical policies. We need to think about ecosocialist policies but we must be flexible in doing so. To move on the debate in this chapter, I try to outline some broad ecosocialist principles and link them to some practical examples of ecosocialist policies. For all the reasons outlined above, some modesty is necessary. There will never be a convincing blueprint for survival and socialism, of whatever shade, should not be constructed by a committee.

ECOLOGY

One essential principle is, of course, ecology. Ecosocialist policies must be based on what works ecologically; although this might seem a rather obvious point, as we have seen in previous chapters, current environmental policies, particularly as regards climate change, are based primarily on what works for the existing capitalist economy, not what is beneficial to the environment or humanity. Conservation of resources and habitats must seek to maintain a diversity of species. Ecological principles demand attention to the idea of usufruct, that is, of leaving the environment in at least as good a form as we found it in the first place.

An excellent example of where ecological principles must be urgently applied is agriculture. In the current system, the maximum production of agricultural commodities for sale is the rule. We have an increasingly globalised agricultural system where crops are produced in one part of the world and shipped or increasingly flown to another part. Huge economics of scale can be gained by specialised production in a particular part of the world. Agricultural commodity-broking firms like Cargill and Archer Daniels Midland are keen to buy the cheapest crops, forcing farmers to cut prices, putting small farmers out of business and shifting cultivation to parts of the world with the lowest wages (Kneen 2002). Also, agricultural production is hugely dependent on fossil fuels, because of petroleum-based fertilizers and pesticides, mechanisation and transport costs.

An ecosocialist alternative would seek to produce food locally to meet local needs. If farming is based on ecological approaches, soil quality can be preserved, energy use reduced and sustainability increased. Ecosocialist agriculture should be organic and based on permaculture, an approach which uses ecological principles to reduce the workload and energy inputs. Crop diversity is important: if there is a diversity of crops, this reduces the likelihood of disease and crops can be used that are suited to local conditions. The use of organic waste can reduce weeds by mulching, conserve water by reducing evaporation, and fertilise crops. Companion planting

discourages pests. A simple example is the intercropping of
onions with carrots: the carrot fly cannot detect its prey,
which it locates by smell, because of the scent of the onions.
Permaculture is a form of landscape design that looks at food
production in a wider perspective and is not narrowly focused
on the present fossil-fuelled monoculture.

There are already examples of ecosocialists creating
or preserving ecological agricultural systems. In Cuba,
permaculture is widely practiced and has made the country
largely self-sufficient in fruit and vegetables in cities and
towns. Unused land in towns and cities has been turned
into community permaculture gardens. This policy was a
result of Cuba's loss of cheap oil, which it used to import
from the Soviet Union. When the Soviet Union collapsed in
1991, the cheap oil disappeared. The pain was felt in the
food sector more than any other and many Cubans suffered
severe hardship. Solidarity activists from Australia introduced
the concept of permaculture and an experimental rooftop
permaculture garden was established. This was deemed to be
a success and the practices very quickly caught on. Initially at
least, it was inspired by need not ecological values and Cuba
still imports most of its food. This is partly because many
essentials, such as wheat to make bread, cannot be grown in
Cuba's tropical climate. Though Cuban agriculture is not fully
organic, the policy has been highly successful. Roberto Perez,
the Cuban ecosocialist thinker and activist who has nurtured
the policy, is a keen advocate of ecosocialist economics and
politics. His ideas have clearly had a strong influence on
Cuban policies for energy, food and environmental protection.

Across the globe in West Bengal, another ecosocialist has
been working for an ecological agricultural system. The
scientist Dr Debal Deb has set up a research institute and

small organic farm to maintain genetic diversity and to preserve traditional ecological forms of agriculture. In India, traditional agriculture is condemned by many politicians and scientists as 'backward' and inefficient. Most farmers buy seeds from large agribusiness firms, and such dependence has made them more reliant on fertilisers and pesticides, sold by the same firms. The lure of short-term productivity and profit has led many farmers into debt and caused a spate of suicides in India (*Independent* 2009). Deb has noted that the agribusiness model has led to an astonishing drop in biological diversity, with thousands of strains of rice being replaced by just a few (Deb 2009: 322). As well as cataloguing different crops, he has organised a seed exchange where farmers can swap seeds, reduce their dependency on agribusiness, and help promote greener agriculture.

Agriculture is closely linked to ecosocialist approaches to waste management. As we have noted, one of the most potent greenhouse gases is methane produced from organic waste. Rubbish creation eats into scarce resources and dumping of waste degrades the environment. Ecosocialists are keen advocates of the zero-waste approach. If goods are made to last longer and can be easily mended, the river of rubbish will be reduced to just a trickle. Organic waste can be composted and instead of being a source of pollution can add to the soil the nutrients needed for ecological agriculture. Recycling is part of the process, but if less waste is produced in the first place, this is even better.

Recycling is another area where Cuba leads the way when it comes to practical ecosocialism:

> The Cuban recycling experience contrasts dramatically with U.S. practices, where local government recycling usually comes only in

direct response to the loss of landfill sites, reinforced by a growing public awareness, and is marred by lack of industry use of what has been collected. Recycling is far better organized and more nearly complete in Cuba, where the population now mines the waste stream for any useful material. From banana peels to toothpaste caps, everything possible is reused. (Brodine 1992)

OPEN-SOURCE ECOSOCIALISM

Given that such policies dealing with waste and farming are shared by virtually all Greens and have no specifically ecosocialist content, why does one need to be a red-green? Surely green on its own is enough? There are NGOs such as Greenpeace who are keen to promote zero waste, and organic groups such as the Soil Association in Britain keen to support non-fossil-fuel farming. However, both these issues and many other environmental policies are dependent on questions of property rights and ownership. Capitalist corporations are very keen to shape agricultural and waste policies in a profitable but far from environmentally friendly direction. With privatisation, corporations control waste disposal: if there is zero waste, they make zero profits. While it is possible to run composting businesses, if composting is achieved in the back garden or by a community project, such businesses suffer. Corporations have been keen to stress the principle of incineration: burning rubbish can be made into a highly profitable business involving large investment projects and contracts that lock rubbish producers into long-term payment plans. Incineration discourages the rational use of waste: if it can be taken away and burnt, why bother. If zero waste were achieved, local authorities would be unable to fulfil their contractual requirements to the incinerating companies.

Incineration is also very damaging to the environment, although the most modern incinerators may not produce deadly dioxins, *if* they are run with care, but this is a big 'if'. However, incinerators remain dangerous. They produce minute, deadly particles, which are a severe threat to human health. Incinerators also produce highly toxic ash that must be dealt with (Thompson and Anthony 2009). In a profit-based system where corporations control rubbish, environmental policies will be watered down and avoided. Environmental rhetoric is used to justify incineration, which has been repackaged as a process of generating energy, although most incinerators produce trivial amounts of electricity.

Agriculture introduces the same issues of property rights, profit and power. Agribusiness influences government policies, drives global institutions such as the World Trade Organization, and uses powerful advertising to shape farming. To practice green alternatives, communities need access to land. Yet land is continually enclosed, transferred from poorer members of the community to elites. In Britain, much of this process was achieved in 1066 when the Norman invaders stole land. Medieval commons continued to exist on marginal land but in the last few centuries they have been largely enclosed and appropriated by a small number of private landlords. The very fact that private landownership is impossible in Cuba allows the community and small farmers the freedom to grow food. Under usufruct rights, farmers can take unused land and grow what they like, but land cannot be sold on to monopolistic corporations.

Clearly, property rights are a key element of the ecosocialist approach. If the correct property rights are in place, policies that promote equity and maintain ecology are more likely to occur. Various forms of private and corporate property rights, where land, for example, is owned and can be exploited by a single user, dominate our planet. Ecosocialism is founded on the principle of common property rights, which allow individuals free access to a resource as long as they don't damage it. For example, even in Britain virtually all beaches are commons; even where a beach has a private owner, individuals can use the beach as long as they don't pollute or damage it. Capitalism restricts access so it can sell us resources which were previously free. By restricting access – access to things we need – poverty is created. Because of such blocked access, wasteful duplication is created. Common access property rights are a way of increasing real prosperity while reducing resource use. Because they are based on use that does not damage a resource, they have a built-in ecological principle.

Ecosocialism is to a large extent a battle over property rights. Genetic diversity has been a commons but corporations aim to patent seeds, so they can profit. Such enclosure increases poverty and is ecologically damaging. Creating legal property rights that give access is both revolutionary and quite modest.

The key commons are land and information. Huge battles over property rights are occurring and to a surprising extent being won by those who advocate the commons. Indigenous people as we have already noted generally maintain communal property rights and battle to preserve and extend them. On the World Wide Web, free software advocates battle to create or preserve information commons.

Building socialist solutions based upon the commons, Venezuela has launched the 'Bolivarian computer' built with open-source software to enable better access: 'The price of other similar brands is US$ 930, and the price of our computer is almost 40% less. But, in addition, it has an added value, given that it comes with open-source software and a three year guarantee, while other brands only offer one year' stated President Hugo Chavez (Paul 2007).

There are elements of an ecosocialist society that require planning and coordination. While much energy provision could occur in a local and decentralised way, the construction of renewable energy systems would require state-level intervention. Equally, rail systems need to be planned nationally and internationally to function well. Regulation aimed at eliminating toxic substances is also necessary. Clearly, an ecosocialist state is necessary, but the conception of the state as an alternative to the market needs to be developed with some care.

This introduces another necessary principle of ecosocialism that is linked to ecology and alternative property rights: the drive for real democracy. In our present society, liberal democracy has become increasingly hollow; there is a very widespread feeling that most individuals have little say in decision making.

Corporate interests increasingly control policy making, by funding political parties, controlling the media and excluding alternative visions. To a lesser or greater extent, the diminishing of formal democracy is almost universal on our planet. Democracy is about power. Power is largely a factor of economic forces, and those with economic power have far more influence, as we have already noted, over the policy process than those who do not.

Direct democracy and redistribution of economic resources are vitally important to the creation of an ecosocialist society. Such a society should be self-managed. The theme of self-management rests on the free association of labour, that is, that workers should own the means of production and make

decisions regarding production. This may sound unrealisti-
cally radical but already in Britain, mutuals and partnerships
are businesses based on worker-based ownership. The John
Lewis Group, which runs one of Britain's supermarkets,
shares all its profits not with shareholders, but with the
workers, who own the partnership. John Lewis is an imperfect
institution and, because it operates within a wider capitalist
market, its existence as a living example of ecosocialism is
rather limited. None the less, it does illustrate the practicality
of worker ownership even in a society dominated by capital.

There are other examples. Cooperatives exist in many parts
of the world and provide democratic ways of producing and
distributing goods and services. New commons-based forms
of peer-to-peer production are also growing.

ECONOMIC DEMOCRACY

Workers' plans are also vital to the creation of an ecosocialist
society. There are numerous industries that are polluting,
wasteful and dangerous. The perceived conflict between
environmental, other ethical considerations and employment
can be exploited to prevent progress. The solution involves
conversion of environmentally destructive industries into
positive alternatives. For example, many of the engineering
skills used to make weapons systems could be used to build
wind energy generators. Democratic control of production
could allow workers to plan for alternative production.

One example is the Lucas Aerospace project of the 1970s.
Under threat from job losses, the workers at Lucas put
together an alternative plan, which came up with ideas for
goods they could produce using their existing skills and

equipment. The aim was to plan to produce goods that were useful to society, rather than the military equipment the company sold to NATO. The list of potential goods is impressive and gives a good idea of the creative potential of the Lucas Aerospace workers. Planned products included medical equipment, renewable energy and clean transport:

- Expanded production of kidney dialysis machines, which Lucas already built, together with research into more portable models.
- Manufacture of a life-support system for use in ambulances, based on a design by a former Lucas engineer turned medical doctor.
- Development of a mobility aid for children with spina bifida. The 'Hobcart', as it was called, was actually designed and built by Lucas workers and advance orders for several thousand units were received ...
- Efficient wind-turbines, drawing on existing expertise in aerodynamics.
- Solar cells and heat pumps
- The 'Power Pack' which coupled a small internal combustion engine to a stack of batteries to create cars with 80% less emissions and 50% greater fuel economy.
- An efficient method for small scale electricity generation for use in the developing world.
- A vehicle like a train but with pneumatic tyres allowing it also to travel on roads. Such a vehicle could navigate inclines of 1 in 6, compared with 1 in 80 for a conventional train, offering a huge potential saving against the need to build tunnels or make deep cuttings to lay rails. A prototype was successfully tested on a railway line in East Kent. (Marsden 2009)

The Lucas workers' plan was ignored, jobs lost and military production continued. In 2008, workers at Visteon, who made plastic parts for Ford cars, occupied their factory in North London, when their business was closed. They believed that they could use their skills to plan for green production, and their campaign leaflet put forward such ideas, noting:

> As well as proper redundancy payments, some are suggesting that the skills of the workers who can make anything in plastic, should be used to make increasingly needed parts for green products – bike and trailer parts, solar panels, turbines, etc. Government investment in this rather than throwing money at bankers could be profitable & save jobs in the long term. (Wall 2009b)

This was not to be; although their occupation did result in their being paid the redundancy they were owed.

Giving trade unions more power is essential and of course, ecosocialists need to be active in the trade union movement, pressing for alternative production rather than jobs from destruction.

An ecosocialist society is likely to see a reduction in formal work, an increased emphasis on the value of traditional undervalued domestic labour and an increasing blurring of the distinction between work and leisure. As Joel Kovel has noted, ecosocialism must also be a form of feminism (2007: 204).

An ecosocialist future would be based on care. In our present society, the highest pay goes to those who work in the esoteric world of hedge funds, derivatives, foreign currency exchange. Jobs that would be lost in an ecosocialist society, currency speculation would not occur if there were controls on currency, as used to be the case, just a generation ago. If economic activity were carried out via mutuals and other worker-controlled projects, shares would disappear. Perhaps the bankers could be retrained to look after their elderly relatives or their children, or to support those in society who may need help because of disability. Unfortunately, the vicious world of finance might not produce the kind of empathy and compassion appropriate for the necessity of care. Caring is one of the most important functions in society but is utterly devalued at present; ecosocialism should be about turning the world upside down and making caring the most valued function in society.

An ecosocialist future would be one without nuclear weapons. Implicit in all of the literature produced by ecosocialists is opposition to nuclear weapons. The US and Russia still have huge arsenals that could kill the world's population many times over. Nuclear weapons have proliferated to nine more countries, including Israel, while even more countries have expressed an interest in acquiring their own nuclear arsenals. The very existence of nuclear weapons, even if they are not used, is a threat. For example, the mining of uranium for nuclear weapons is a polluting process, often involving assaults on the land rights of indigenous people.

The transportation, storage and eventual disposal of nuclear weapons all provide grave risks to humanity. There is almost a news blackout on the terrible danger of nuclear submarines, vessels that are propelled by nuclear reactors while carrying nuclear missiles. Some have sunk, with the loss of life of those on board, while the hulks lie rotting, like radioactive time bombs, at the bottom of the world's oceans. Vigorous efforts to promote universal nuclear disarmament are necessary. Nuclear weapons are of course part of a framework of military capitalism. They are used to threaten those who challenge capitalist logic and provide a tidy profit for arms manufacturers. The process of workers-based plans for alternative production will face a particular challenge transforming nuclear weapons production to something that supports life instead of death.

Ecosocialists oppose nuclear power, a technology that is closely linked to nuclear weapons production. Nuclear accidents have the potential to kill millions and, as with nuclear weapons, the entire process from fuelling to waste disposal is highly dangerous. Nuclear energy has no place in ecosocialist energy plans. As we have noted, renewable energy can meet our needs together with serious policies to combat climate change by reducing energy demand.

An ecosocialist future will be one that respects other species. The idea that the rest of nature can be used as a tool for human benefit is inappropriate. A measure of animal rights also brings benefits to human beings. The worst assaults on animals for factory farming and vivisection do not occur because of a desire to benefit humanity through cheaper food or more effective medicines, but to make profit. Factory farming is not only cruel but generates highly polluting waste products; the methane from massive factory-farming projects contributes to climate change. The packing of animals together in a confined space spreads disease, which in turn leads to excessive use of antibiotics and antivirals. Such use tends to breed ever-stronger disease strains, such as avian bird flu, that threaten humanity (Davis 2006). While vivisection may have its defenders, it rests on the difficult argument that other species are biologically similar enough to human beings to make it scientifically valid, but morally so different from our species that such experiments are ethically acceptable. In the field of health, pharmaceutical companies develop new medicines so they can enjoy monopoly profits for patenting them; this duplication fuels health-care bankruptcy and animal abuse. Animal rights throws up some dilemmas. Traditionally the left have often ignored animal rights issues; those most concerned to respect other species are often indigenous people, who believe such respect is consistent with hunting. While the issue of animal rights may be a difficult area, for both moral reasons and practical, an ecosocialist politics is inadequate if it does not include animal liberation.

Nearly all societies are facing a growing number of social problems; these include obesity, crime and family breakdown, which are caused to large extent by social inequality. Using meticulous research, Richard Wilkinson and Kate Pickett have established the surprising fact that inequality is socially damaging, even to the rich. While this should not unduly worry those of us who are not billionaires, it does illustrate the destructive and pervasive results of inequality. The more unequal a society, the greater the social problems, including mental and physical ill health:

> The US is wealthier and spends more on health care than any other country, yet a baby born in Greece, where average income levels are about half that of the US, has a lower risk of infant mortality and longer life expectancy than an American baby. Obesity is twice as common in the UK as the more equal societies of Sweden and Norway, and six times more common in the US than in Japan. Teenage birth rates are six times higher in the UK than in more equal societies; mental illness is three times as common in the US as in Japan; murder rates are three times higher in more unequal countries. The examples are almost endless.
>
> Inequality, it seems, is an equal-opportunity disease, something that has a direct impact on everyone. (Crace 2009)

Pickett and Wilkinson's book *The Spirit Level* is a powerful account of the immense social as well as environment damage created by capitalism. Wealth is not gained from the simple accumulation of the results of hard work; it is a product of ownership. Share ownership is most significant: increasingly, a small number of people controlling a large number of shares get the rest of us to work for them. Moving to a society based on mutual ownership would be a very effective way of redistributing wealth and income. Once again, property rights are key.

An ecosocialist health-care system would be necessary. Eliminating the most serious sources of pollution would help, so, as the findings of *The Spirit Level* suggest, would be creating a more equal society. Free health care may seem utopian in some parts of the world. Yet in Britain, even though the country had just emerged from war, the Attlee government of 1945 constructed the National Health Service, a free health-care system based on need. Today, the NHS is very much under attack in Britain from those seeking to privatise it, but still provides a model for the rest of the world. Ecosocialist health is about prevention and participation. Cuba also provides an excellent model of how health care can be provided. Prevention, together with changes to patent laws that currently allow pharmaceutical companies to make huge monopoly profits on drugs, would also be important in creating a healthier society.

TRANSITIONS

Policies need to be linked to strategy. Political parties have already been elected on radical red-green platforms but have often achieved rather limited results. The notion that a political party can win votes and suddenly transform society is unrealistic; an elected political party will face very difficult challenges in implementing its policies. Green parties have elected members of parliament and participated in governments. However, these victories have so far taken place within the context of broader coalitions. While red-green governments, made up of Green and Social Democratic parties, have occurred in countries such as France, Belgium, Sweden and Germany, the policy gains have been limited. The German Greens dropped most of their anti-capitalist critique, before participating in government with the Social Democrats. They phased out nuclear power and now Germany is a major producer of renewable energy; however, more radical policies were eroded, with the Greens supporting NATO and the invasion of Afghanistan. The decision of the Greens to support the war in Kosovo was a particular turning-point. This process also affects more specifically red-green parties such as the Norwegian Socialist Left Party; while this party is part of a governing coalition and has done much to introduce environmental reforms in the country, Norway is still one of the world major oil producers and as such drives climate change. Red-green policies demand profound transformation, but the political system tends to fade bright colours.

One approach to achieving change is to construct transitional policies, the kind of revolutionary reforms that tend to nurture greater positive change when introduced. In countries where ecosocialists have been elected, they tend to be minorities in parties themselves, which are in turn minorities within the party political system. While a kind of red-green politics that allows participation in government has emerged in several European countries, there is still huge pressure to maintain policies based on capitalist growth. Thus developing transitional policies is especially important so that real progress towards ecosocialism can be made, rather than reforming an unsustainable and unjust system so it can continue a little longer.

Transitional policies need to be debated and developed and different specific policies will be appropriate in different parts of the world and will depend upon the varied circumstances ecosocialists find themselves. I have produced a list of my own favoured transitional policies which I hope will stimulate further discussion:

1) Defending indigenous control of rainforests and other vital ecosystems
2) Allowing workers to take control of bankrupt businesses
3) Using government bailouts to mutualise resources
4) Arms and SUV conversion as an essential element of a Green New Deal
5) Legislating for open-source patenting
6) Land reform
7) Massive funding for libraries and other forms of social sharing
8) A tax and welfare system to support commons
9) Competition reform to transform ownership
10) Social ownership of pharmaceuticals and medicine.

(Wall 2009c: 188)

Many of these reforms are aimed at creating commons-based property rights; such property rights would create the framework for an ecosocialist society. Measures such as indigenous control of key ecosystems and conversion of industries to produce renewable energy and other green technologies would be vital to combat climate change. These reforms would act as revolutionary reforms which would tend to lead to greater change. They would, of course, be strongly resisted by a host of vested corporate interests.

The Second Ecosocialist International Network meeting in Belém, Brazil outlined four essential ecosocialist policy areas; they provide a good summary of the discussions here:

Firstly, the energy system, by replacing carbon-based fuels and biofuels with clean sources of power under community control: wind, geothermal, wave, and above all, solar power.

Secondly, the transportation system, by drastically reducing the use of private trucks and cars, replacing them with a free and efficient public transportation.

Thirdly, present patterns of production, consumption, and building, which are based on waste, inbuilt obsolescence, competition and pollution, by producing only sustainable and recyclable goods and developing green architecture.

Fourthly, food production and distribution, by defending local food sovereignty as far as possible, eliminating polluting industrial agribusinesses, creating sustainable agro-ecosystems and working to renew soil fertility. (Fuentes 2009)

It would be possible to continue such discussion of the policies appropriate to an ecosocialist society. However, highly detailed blueprints for ecosocialism are counter-productive; the blueprint will grow organically through debate and participation. We will make the path by walking it. The key task is to build an ecosocialist movement as a means of slowing and reversing the capitalist assault on our planet. Chapter 4 looks at the international origins, growth and development of the diverse and increasingly dynamic global green left.

4
The Ecosocialist Challenge

Marxists could take their inspiration from Marx's remarks on the Paris Commune: workers cannot take possession of the capitalist state apparatus and put it to function at their service. They have to 'break it' and replace it by a radically different, democratic and non-statist form of political power. The same applies, mutatis mutandis, to the productive apparatus: by its nature, its structure, it is not neutral, but at the service of capital accumulation and the unlimited expansion of the market. It is in contradiction with the needs of environment-protection and with the health of the population. One must therefore 'revolutionize' it, in a process of radical trans-formation. This may mean, for certain branches of production, to discontinue them: for instance, nuclear plants, certain methods of mass/industrial fishing (responsible for the extermination of several species in the seas), the destructive logging of tropical forests, etc (the list is very long!). In any case, the productive forces, and not only the relations of production, have to be deeply changed

– to begin with, by a revolution in the energy-system, with the replacement of the present sources – essentially fossil – responsible for the pollution and poisoning of the environment, by renewable ones: water, wind, sun. Of course, many scientific and technological achievements of modernity are precious, but the whole productive system must be transformed.

Löwy 2009

4. William Morris (William Morris Society)

The Ecosocialist International Network (EIN) was launched in October 2007 at a meeting in the mayor's office of Montreuil, a small suburb of Paris. It brought together over

50 activists from as far afield as Australia, Canada and Brazil. In January 2009, the EIN held its second meeting at the World Social Forum in Belém in Brazil, with a strong showing from indigenous, left and green activists mainly from Latin America. Established to create a global ecosocialist movement, the network was directly inspired by the Ecosocialist Manifesto. This document was written by Michael Löwy, a Brazilian member of the Fourth International, and Professor Joel Kovel, a New York socialist who ran for the Green Party's US presidential nomination. The origins of the Ecosocialist Manifesto, co-written by Löwy, a member of a socialist international and Kovel, a member of the Green Party, reflect the mission of ecosocialism, to make Greens redder and reds green. However, ecosocialism has wider and deeper roots than the EIN. It is possible to trace ecosocialism back to Marx and beyond.

MARX AND ENGELS ON ECOLOGY

While Marx is often dismissed as an anti-environmental thinker, there are constant reminders in his work and that of his co-author Frederick Engels of ecological themes. Indeed, Engels' early works included *The Condition of the English Working Class*, which examined how industrial pollution poisoned workers and the environment. John Bellamy Foster's book *Marx's Ecology* notes that environmental concern is found throughout Marx's writings and that the concept of ecology, although Marx did not use the term, is essential to his thought (2000). Foster argues that Marx's notion of a 'metabolic rift' between humanity and the rest of nature is a vital ecological insight. During the twentieth century, as more of Marx's work was published, the notion of a greener Marx was strengthened. In his *Paris Manuscripts*, he refers to the dangers of a humanity alienated from the rest of nature; ecological themes are also important in the *Grundrisse*, his unpublished plan for a lifetime project, which was to include *Capital* as well as volumes on land, the state and other aspects of society and economy. Although often forgotten by both the left and environmentalists, Marx's and Engels' best-known works, have powerful ecological sentiments.

It's worth quoting, even at some length, a statement from Engels, which suggests a key understanding of ecology and the idea that divisions between humanity and the rest of nature are ultimately artificial:

Let us not, however, flatter ourselves overmuch on account of our human victories over nature. For each such victory nature takes its revenge on us. Each victory, it is true, in the first place brings about the results we expected, but in the second and third places it has quite different, unforeseen effects which only too often cancel the first. The people who, in Mesopotamia, Greece, Asia Minor and elsewhere, destroyed the forests to obtain cultivable land, never dreamed that by removing along with the forests the collecting centres and reservoirs of moisture they were laying the basis for the present forlorn state of those countries. When the Italians of the Alps used up the pine forests on the southern slopes, so carefully cherished on the northern slopes, they had no inkling that by doing so they were cutting at the roots of the dairy industry in their region; they had still less inkling that they were thereby depriving their mountain springs of water for the greater part of the year, and making it possible for them to pour still more furious torrents on the plains during the rainy seasons. Those who spread the potato in Europe were not aware that with these farinaceous tubers they were at the same time spreading scrofula. Thus at every step we are reminded that we by no means rule over nature like a conqueror over a foreign people, like someone standing outside nature – but that we, with flesh, blood and brain, belong to nature, and exist in its midst, and that all our mastery of it consists in the fact that we have the advantage over all other creatures of being able to learn its laws and apply them correctly.

And, in fact, with every day that passes we are acquiring a better understanding of these laws and getting to perceive both the more immediate and the more remote consequences of our interference with the traditional course of nature. In particular, after the mighty advances made by the natural sciences in the present century, we are more than ever in a position to realize, and hence to control, also the more remote natural consequences of at least our day-to-day production activities. But the more this progresses the more will men not only feel but also know their oneness with nature, and the more impossible will become the senseless and unnatural idea of a contrast between mind and matter, man and nature, soul and body, such as arose after the decline of classical antiquity in Europe and obtained its highest elaboration in Christianity. (Engels 1987: 459–60)

While Engels used the term 'victories over nature', it is clear from his writings that he saw this phrase as problematic, both because to benefit from nature we must respect nature and, more fundamentally, it is wrong to see human beings as separate from nature. Marx and Engels were fascinated by the natural sciences, including biology. John Bellamy Foster argues in great and convincing detail that ecological themes were an essential part of Marx's thought, from his early work as a student studying Greek philosophy through to his final works. There are many myths about Marx and the environment: although he was a dialectical thinker who saw the growth of a working class within capitalism as key to the creation of communism, much of what has been written about his supposed anti-environmental views is simply false. For example, he and Engels are accused of seeing labour as the only source of economic value and ignoring the value of the rest of nature; however, they identify nature as a source of value as well. The Canadian writer David Orton has suggested 'Deeper Greens not only see Nature as having value in itself but also see Nature as the principal source of human wealth—not labor power as in Marxism.' He was corrected by Frank Rotering, another radical green, who observed that Marx quoted William Petty in relation to wealth – 'labor is its father and the earth its mother' – in *Capital* (Rotering 2006).

A detailed examination of Marx and Engels' ecological thought is provided by John Bellamy Foster. Amongst others, Ted Benton (1993), Paul Burkett (1999), Jonathan Hughes (2000) and David Pepper (1993) have also produced accounts of the affinity between Marx's work and ecological politics. Marx also had an interest in indigenous cultures, which was revealed in a set of notebooks edited in the twentieth century by Lawrence Krader (Krader 1972).

NEWS FROM NOWHERE

While we often forget that Marx was an ecologist, it is equally common to forget that the best-known British political ecologist, William Morris, was a Marxist. Morris was a poet, designer and conservationist; his concern with the environment and art led him to political activism as a socialist. Together with Engels, and Marx's daughter Eleanor, he was active in the Social Democratic Federation, Britain's first socialist political party, established in the 1880s. In numerous articles, pamphlets and the utopian novel *News from Nowhere*, he advocated an ecosocialist politics in all but name (Thompson 1976). He argued that environmental destruction and exploitation of workers were both driven by the process of capital accumulation. Morris believed only revolution could free the earth and humanity from bondage. His concern for the environment is clear throughout his work; typically, writing in the essay 'Art and Socialism', he stated that no one should be able to 'cut down, for mere profit, trees whose loss would spoil a landscape: neither on any pretext should people be allowed to darken the daylight with smoke, to befoul rivers, or to degrade any spot of earth with squalid litter and brutal wasteful disorder' (Morris 2004: 15–16).

Similar views were held by a number of late Victorian and Edwardian socialist writers in Britain. One of the most remarkable was Edward Carpenter. A member of the Sheffield Socialist Society and an openly gay man, Carpenter was a hero to the larger socialist movement in Britain. On his eightieth birthday in 1924, the entire membership of the first Labour Party Cabinet, then governing Britain, signed his birthday card (Edward Carpenter Archive, n.d.).

Carpenter was a radical democrat, virtually an anarchist; he advocated the liberation of women and was a vegetarian who supported animal rights. From 1880 through to the First World War in 1914, an early green movement in Britain overlapped with socialist and anarchist currents. The author Peter Gould, in his book *Early Green Politics*, has provided a detailed study, doing for British socialism between 1884 and 1905 what Foster has done for Marx and Engels, namely, revealing a largely forgotten green politics (Gould 1988). The novelist E.M. Forster described Carpenter as a socialist in the tradition of Blake and Shelley (1951: 213). The Romantic poets, for example, Blake and Shelley, were concerned to challenge both the exploitation of humanity and nature, were hostile to slavery and land enclosure, and advocated a republic based on common ownership and democracy. Poems like Blake's 'Auguries of Innocence' make statements that all ecosocialists can applaud:

> A robin redbreast in a cage
> Puts all heaven in a rage.
>
> A dove-house fill'd with doves and pigeons
> Shudders hell thro' all its regions.
> A dog starv'd at his master's gate
> Predicts the ruin of the state.
>
> (Blake 1977: 507)

GREEN LEFT LENIN?

Such early green politics, a green politics that was in essence ecosocialist, was not confined to Britain. Indeed as Weiner (2000: 27) has shown, there were powerful ecological currents in the Bolshevik Party and Lenin took a personal interest in conservation. After the Russian Revolution, nature reserves were established in the Soviet Union and scientific ecology flourished. The leading Bolshevik, Bukharin, who at one time rivalled both Stalin and Trotsky in influence, wrote *Philosophical Arabesque*, a powerful book which included ecological insights (2005).

In Germany during the 1920s, the magazine *Urania* also put forward ecosocialist ideas (Hülsberg 1988: 5). In 1928, the German Marxist theorist Walter Benjamin rejected the 'imperial domination' of nature in his book *One-Way Street* (1985). Similar ecosocialist currents and sentiment can be found in the US and in other European countries between 1920 and 1960.

John Bellamy Foster has done some very interesting work showing that ecologists interested in socialism and socialists concerned with ecology were active, although often forgotten, throughout the twentieth century. A number of important scientific figures who developed biology and ecology as disciplines had red credentials. He notes that Rachel Carson, author of the iconic book *Silent Spring* which revealed the danger of pesticides, was a woman of the progressive left (Foster 2009: 67).

However, during much of the twentieth century, the green element in socialist politics was largely forgotten. Stalinism dominated Marxist politics, and various forms of Fabian reformism influenced the centre-left, social-democratic alternatives to Stalin. The Fabians were a group who believed in gradual but certain path towards socialism, rejecting revolution for what they saw as a strengthening wave of reforms.

Despite their origins in a group called 'The Fellowship of the New Life', which was linked to Edward Carpenter, the Fabians were rather elitist and technocratic, having little time for grassroots projects or the creative potential of the public (Pease 1916). Both Fabianism and Stalinism saw socialism primarily as about increasing industrial development and centralising power via a bureaucratic elite. Neither Fabianism nor Stalinism, despite their huge differences, had much concern with the environment.

Stalin suppressed Soviet environmentalism and, during the Lysenko dispute, had many scientists killed or sent to labour camps, for disagreeing with the official and flawed theory of natural adaptation. Although after his death the Soviet Union acknowledged the damaging effects of Stalin's rule, to some extent his brutal assaults on the natural environment continued.

The ecological damage created in the Soviet Union is well known. Chernobyl, the world's worst nuclear disaster, devastated a huge area of Ukraine and left many thousands with cancer. Industrialised cotton production reduced the volume of the Aral Sea by 75 per cent, turning much of the surrounding area into a desert. Eastern Europe, as part of the Soviet bloc, generated acid rain and smog, from burning 'dirty' types of coal (Komarov 1980).

From the left, there were flickers of environmental concern. The Communist Party of Great Britain (CPGB) activist Benny Rothman led the Kinder Scout mass trespasses in the 1930s, in a campaign for working-class access to the Derbyshire moorland for walking and hiking. John Bellamy Foster cites the ecological insights of Christopher Caudwell, another CPGB member of the 1930s who was killed in the Spanish Civil War (2009: 155). The CPGB also promoted more environmentally conscious policies in the 1970s. The Labour government of the 1940s created national parks and indulged in nostalgia for William Morris. However, left politics and green politics diverged for many decades, while left alternatives to social democracy and Stalinism also generally ignored the environment for much of the twentieth century, particularly between the 1920 and 1970s.

While Trotsky was an inspiring political leader who worked to build a new socialist international in opposition to Stalin's tyranny, he was no ecosocialist. Trotsky was a keen advocate of a productivist vision of industrial expansion, with little of the apparent ecological concern of Marx or Engels. In *Literature and Revolution*, Trotsky saw the reshaping of nature by humanity as an artistic endeavour:

... nature will become more 'artificial'. The present distribution of mountains and rivers, of fields, of meadows, of steppes, of forests, and of seashores, cannot be considered final. Man has already made changes in the map of nature that are not few nor insignificant. But they are mere pupils' practice in comparison with what is coming ... Man will occupy himself with re-registering mountains and rivers, and will earnestly and repeatedly make improvements in nature. In the end, he will have rebuilt the earth, if not in his own image, at least according to his own taste. We have not the slightest fear that this taste will be bad.

Through the machine, man in Socialist society will command nature in its entirety, with its grouse and its sturgeons. He will point out places for mountains and for passes. He will change the course of the rivers, and he will lay down rules for the oceans. The idealist simpletons may say that this will be a bore, but that is why they are simpletons. (Trotsky 1955: 252)

Unlike Marx and Engels, Trotsky seems to suggest that humanity is separate from the rest of nature, and should and can master nature easily, with few negative consequences. Even Trotsky's nod to the tiger suggests no real concern with ecology: 'Most likely, thickets and forests and grouse and tigers will remain, but only where man commands them to remain. And man will do it so well that the tiger won't even notice the machine, or feel the change, but will live as he lived in primeval times. The machine is not in opposition to the earth' (ibid.).

Trotsky should not be singled out and condemned. The views he proclaimed were near universal on the left and within other political ideologies for much of the twentieth century. Typically, council communism, while another alternative to Stalinism, seems to have produced little or no literature on the environment. Council communists echoed the notion of socialism as the achievement of blunt mastery over nature. For example, the Dutch council communist Pannekoek writing in 1933 argued:

> On the basis of Marxism which sees the development of society as a succession of forms of production, it sees a long and hard annexation of humanity on the basis of the development of labour, of tools and of forms of labour towards an ever increasing productivity ... And in each period of development, the proletariat finds characteristics which are related to its own nature ... In capitalism: the knowledge of nature, the priceless development of natural science which allowed man, through technology, to dominate nature and its own fate. (Pannekoek 1933)

With the decline of the early forms of ecosocialism, right-wing and fascist forms of ecological politics grew in strength; for example, in Britain, Rolf Gardiner sought to fight environmental degradation and struck up a friendship with Hitler's agriculture minister Walther Darre. Gardiner started as a guild socialist, an approach that built on Morris's politics to advocate a decentralized and environmentally conscious form of workers' control, but he rapidly moved to the far right. He was not alone: other former guild socialists became what can crudely be termed 'ecofascists'. For example, A.J. Penty, who wrote *The Restoration of the Gild System* in 1906, became a supporter of Mussolini. Indeed, the organic agriculture group, the Soil Association, counted amongst its early members Jorian Jenks, who edited its journal *Mother Earth*. Jenks was a prominent member of the British Union of Fascism in the 1930s and acted as agricultural adviser to its leader Oswald Mosley.

WESTERN MARXISM AND ECOSOCIALISM

Disillusionment with Stalinism led to the growth of various strands of Western Marxism, some of which, in contrast to Trotskyism and council communism, advocated ideas that can be seen as ecosocialist. The Frankfurt School, made up of exiles from Hitler's Germany, helped inspire the creation of both the student movements of the 1960s and the green parties that came into being in the 1970s and '80s.

Adorno and Horkheimer, in *The Dialectic of Enlightenment* (1979), noted that scientific knowledge was used not to liberate but to enslave both humanity and nature. Another member of the Frankfurt School, Herbert Marcuse, argued in *One Dimensional Man* that capitalism exploited workers not only by appropriating their surplus labour power but by chaining them to an alienated consumer society. Marcuse spoke of the dangers of 'aggressive and wasteful use of science and technology' and critiqued what he saw as an 'overdeveloped society' (1966: xi)

Marcuse took part in a Paris seminar on 'Ecology and Revolution' in 1972, arguing that the Vietnam War was an imperialistic assault on both the Vietnamese people and their environment, noting:

> It is no longer enough to do away with people living now; life must also be denied to those who aren't even born yet by burning and poisoning the earth, defoliating the forests, blowing up the dikes. This bloody insanity will not alter the ultimate course of the war but it is a very clear expression of where contemporary capitalism is at: the cruel waste of productive resources in the imperialist homeland goes hand in hand with the cruel waste of destructive forces and consumption of commodities of death manufactured by the war industry. (quoted in Kellner 1982)

One of Marcuse's last essays, 'Ecology and the Critique of Modern Society', written before his death in 1979, dealt with this theme. Douglas Kellner argues that he saw

> ... a contradiction between capitalist productivity and nature, for in its quest for higher profits and the domination of nature, capitalism inevitably destroyed nature. Capitalist production manifested an unleashing of aggressive and destructive energies which destroyed life and polluted nature. In this process, human beings are transformed into tools of labor and become instruments of destruction. Introjecting capitalism's aggressive, competitive, and destructive impulses, individuals themselves engage in ever more virulent destruction of the natural environment and anything (individuals, communities, and nations) which stand in the way of its productive exploitation of resources people, and markets. (ibid.)

The psychoanalyst Erich Fromm drew upon Marx's *Paris Manuscripts* to argue that capitalism threatened human subjectivity, making us alienated and passive. In books such as *To Have or to Be* (1979) and *Marx's Concept of Man* (1961), Fromm advocated a powerful form of ecological socialism. He also noted that Marx's ideas had been misunderstood by many:

> Among all the misunderstandings there is probably none more widespread than the idea of Marx's 'materialism.' Marx is supposed to have believed that the paramount psychological motive in man is his wish for monetary gain and comfort, and that this striving for maximum profit constitutes the main incentive in his personal life and in the life of the human race [... however] Marx's aim was that of the spiritual emancipation of man, of his liberation from the chains of economic determination, of restituting him in his human wholeness, of enabling him to find unity and harmony with his fellow man and with nature. (Fromm 1961: 1)

Western Marxism, in its disillusion with left parties, rejected the role of the working class in achieving socialism; while it looked to new social movements for change, it took an academic approach, preferring to theorize, often at a very abstract level, than to be part of political change and activism. Even Marcuse, who was more engaged with the student radicals, noted his own relative separation from real political engagement. Marcuse and the other Frankfurt theorists did not try to build parties, networks, or social movement. The involvement of other Western Marxists – as varied as Althusser, Sartre, or Goldman – in practical movements for change, was generally rather limited.

John Bellamy Foster is also critical of Western Marxism, including the Frankfurt School, for rejecting the study of natural sciences. He suggests that while they rejected the positivism of much of the left, a positivism which suggested that human beings could be examined scientifically with implications of control and inevitability, they also rejected any notion of science as a serious tool of socialist liberation. This rejection, while based on a well-founded distrust of authoritarian forms of socialism, is problematic for a number of reasons. It suggests that humanity is separate from the rest of nature and it downgrades an examination of scientific ecology, which is needed to deal with severe environmental problems.

ECOSOCIALIST PIONEERS

However, some individuals promoted a left green or ecosocialist politics. While he rejected the term, a key figure in the development of ecosocialism in the second half of the twentieth century was the American writer Murray Bookchin. Brought up in New York, Bookchin became politically active in his teens in the 1930s, moving from the Communist Party to Trotskyism and then on to anarchism (White 2008). In the 1950s, Bookchin, using the pseudonym Lewis Herber, wrote *Our Synthetic Environment*, which illustrated the environmental ill effects of various pollutants and pesticides. During his long career, he developed a detailed political philosophy of social ecology. While he drew on Marx's criticism of capitalism, he was highly critical in turn of Marxist political parties, which he saw as manipulative and sectarian. Bookchin was a keen and aggressive polemicist who attacked alternative currents of green, socialist and anarchist thought with vigour. Paradoxically, his theoretical work has, given his rejection of socialism, been important to the development of ecosocialism. For example, he was critical of Greens who failed to recognise the destructive effects of capitalism on the environment. After becoming interested in green politics, Joel Kovel, co-author of *The Ecosocialist Manifesto* (Kovel and Löwy 2001), initially worked with Bookchin. The latter also created a Green Left Network in the US Green Party, which Kovel was involved with (Kovel 1998: 54), before he fell out with Bookchin over his perceived sectarianism. Bookchin's books on social ecology, such as *Post-scarcity Anarchism* (1971) and *Toward an Ecological Society* (1974), are still classics of green anti-capitalist thought. On the other side of the Atlantic, the British historian E.P. Thompson was equally important to the development of ecosocialism. Thompson, famous for books including the classic *The Making of the English Working Class* (1991), left the Communist Party in 1956 because of the Soviet Union's invasion of Hungary. Instead of retreating into academic work like much of the Western Marxist tradition, or embracing small group dogmatism, Thompson worked to create a New Left, based on democratic ideas and practice. He helped found the *New Left Review*, and most significantly worked to restore the reputation of William Morris, who by the 1950s was in danger of being forgotten. Thompson published a biography of Morris (1976), and wrote extensively about William Blake and a tradition of English radicals who advocated environmental and socialist ideas. He was also an activist and in the 1980s threw himself into reviving the peace movement in Britain through the Campaign for Nuclear Disarmament. He also helped create the organisation European Nuclear Disarmament to establish links between peace activists in Western and Eastern Europe. I was lucky enough to hear him speak at an Ecology Party conference in 1982 in Britain. Ecological concern was important to his vision of socialism but above all, he worked to halt the accelerating nuclear weapons build-up in the 1980s that threatened catastrophe.

The Welsh literary theorist Raymond Williams worked with Thompson and like him sought a politics that was both plural and open but revolutionary. He published a pamphlet entitled 'Ecology and Socialism', which helped accelerate ecosocialist politics in Britain in the 1980s, although regrettably he seemed largely dismissive of the ecological strains of thought in Marx's and Engels' work. Much of this essay and his much larger body of work remains inspiring today. Williams argued in 1982: 'We can see that in local, national and international terms, there are already kinds of thinking which can become the elements of an ecologically conscious socialism. We can begin to think of a new kind of social analysis in which ecology and economics become, as they always should be, a single science' (Williams 1989: 225).

By the 1980s, green parties were established in many parts of the globe, although most particularly in Western Europe. Both the student protest movements of the late 1960s and early 1970s and the growth of global environmental concern helped create ecological political parties. Many of these drew from the right as well as the left. For example, in Britain a key thinker was Edward Goldsmith, editor of *The Ecologist* magazine, who praised conservative notions of the nuclear family and challenged the left. Many socialists vigorously attacked the green movement, seeing it as an outgrowth of an elite concern to conserve the environment for those with wealth and power (Enzensberger 1974).

The neo-Malthusian tone of much ecopolitics, that blamed over-population for environmental damage, was seen as reactionary by most on the left. Radical social movements opposed to nuclear power and nuclear weapons fuelled the growth of European green parties. The green parties, especially in France and Germany, were more influenced by anarchism, libertarian left ideas, feminism, peace and demands for social justice than population concern.

The extra-parliamentary left of Germany moved to help form the Greens with a strong Maoist current advocating a redder form of green. In Britain, the Socialist Environmental and Resources Association (SERA) was created by individuals who left the early Ecology Party then known as 'People', because they felt it was too right wing. SERA published Raymond Williams' 'Ecology and Socialism' and in the early 1980s were very important for promoting ecosocialism. SERA was mainly linked to the Labour Party, but included Ecology Party members such as the prominent environmentalist Jonathon Porritt. It was influential in promoting ecological thought to Labour Party activists involved in the Greater

London Council and other municipal left projects during the 1980s. Although SERA still exists, it is now exclusively a body for members of the Labour Party. With the advent of Tony Blair, Labour in turn moved sharply to the right; as a result, while SERA still does important environmental work, the group is less important to ecosocialist thought and action than it was in the 1980s.

During the 1980s in most Western European countries, green parties moved to the left and attracted many who were disillusioned with both Marxist groups and social-democratic, centre-left political parties. A number of key European intellectuals made the case for ecosocialist politics. Rudolf Bahro, an East German Marxist, was exiled to the West after publishing *The Alternative in Eastern Europe* (1981). E.P. Thompson noted that, despite having had no contact with William Morris's work, Bahro developed a vision of transforming East Germany in an ecosocialist direction in the spirit of Morris. Andre Gorz, a French Marxist, wrote *Ecology as Politics* (1980), arguing specifically that a Marxist approach was necessary to explain why society was obsessed with environmentally damaging economic growth.

In retrospect, not all, but much of this movement towards ecosocialism, was a movement away from socialism as much as a movement towards ecology. Andre Gorz entitled one of his books *Farewell to the Working Class* (1982). Bahro, who joined the German Greens and was a prominent member of its most radical fundamentalist wing, entitled one of his essay collections *From Red to Green* (1984). He decisively rejected virtually all of the key elements of Marx's thought.

There are some Green Party members who have seen their involvement as an explicit route away from left politics.

The most famous Green Party 'realos', those who advocate coalition with other parties, participation in government and the abandonment not just of left but environmental radicalism, were once on the far left. Joschka Fischer, who participated in the student protest movement as an anarchist and ended up as German Green Party leader, comes to mind. So does Danny Cohn-Bendit, one of the authors in the 1960s of *Obsolete Communism: The Left Wing Alternative* and a notorious student radical (Cohn-Bendit and Cohn-Bendit 2000). Alain Lipietz, a French Green MEP and a leader of the party, in a thoughtful book on political ecology titled *Green Hopes* (1995), notes his transition from Maoism to a politics that rejects the traditional left. There has thus been a tendency for ecosocialism to be a stepping-stone from socialism to ecology for some on the left. However, despite the deficiencies of much of the twentieth-century left, as we have seen, it is vital to create an ecosocialist movement. Whatever the weaknesses of the left's approach to ecology, it is impossible to explain ecological destruction without reference to the capitalist drive for endless profits and growth. Red and green need to be brought together to solve the ecological crisis.

In the third millennium, ecosocialist organisation and thought has accelerated. Joel Kovel's book *The Enemy of Nature* (2007) is perhaps the most detailed account of the damage capitalism does to the environment, and is a call to create an ecosocialist movement to transform the world, so that we all have a future. In turn, *The Ecosocialist Manifesto*, drafted by Kovel and Michael Löwy (2001), has been used to launch a global ecosocialist network.

ECOSOCIALISM IN AFRICA

Ecosocialism has also rooted in Africa. Marxism, feminism, anti-colonialism and environmental concern are central to the work of the great Kenyan novelist Ngũgĩ in books such as *The Wizard of the Crow*. His imaginary republic of Abruria represents the situation in too many real African countries:

> This forest was now threatened by charcoal, paper, and timber merchants who cut down trees hundreds of years old. When it came to forest, indeed to any natural resource the Abrurian State and big American, European, and Japanese companies, in alliance with the local African, Indian, and European rich, were all united by one slogan: A loot-a continua. They knew how to take but not how to give back to the soil. The unregulated clearing of forests affected the rhythm of the rains, and a semidesert was beginning to creep from the prairie to the hills. (Ngũgĩ wa Thiong'o 2006: 201)

Thomas Sankara can lay claim to being the first ecosocialist leader of an African country, one of very few African leaders who have stood in the way of the 'loot-a-continua'. Such opposition to using politics as a way of making an elite rich from plundering Africans and the African environment probably cost him his life. As leader of Burkina Faso before his assassination in 1987, Sankara introduced ecosocialist policies to conserve the environment and empower peasant farmers in his country. He outlawed female circumcision, opposed apartheid and with the help of Cuban doctors expanded health care in one of the world's poorest countries. His government planted 10 million trees in an effort to stop the spread of the Sahel Desert into the country. His policies were popular with most people in Burkina Faso but he was killed. His assassins still govern Burkina Faso today, supported by grants from the IMF and World Bank (Haywood 2007).

In South Africa, a Green Socialist Coalition was formed in 2008, but failed to contest the presidential election because of the expensive process of official registration. Environmental problems created under apartheid have impacted most on the black population of the sprawling townships and remain severe today. Coal mining is a huge industry in the country and South African coal is exported globally. While the 'dirtiest' coal is burnt in South African power stations, the better grade is sold abroad. The ruling African National Congress have continued with largely free market policies; in response, anti-privatisation movements have arisen which are opposed to high utility bills. A large but fragmented environmental movement exists in South Africa; however, left political parties have until recently shown little interest in the environment. While green parties have elected members of parliament in a number of African states, the South African Green Party has failed to grow or elected candidates to official positions. Typically, in 2004, it gained just 0.21 per cent in the Western Cape, the only region of the country the party contested.

The Green Socialist Coalition was formed by the Operation Khanyisa Movement, which arose out of the Anti-Privatization Forum in Gauteng (the province which includes Johannesburg) and Ecopeace, an independent party in Durban, devoted to protecting the environment. The Ecopeace Party was formed in 1995, using Che Guevara's slogan 'A true revolutionary is motivated by feelings of love.' Residents' associations and left-wing organisations such as the Socialist Group, Keep Left, Socialism from Below, the Democratic Socialist Movement and the Workers Party with links to the Black Consciousness Movement have also joined the coalition:

> Its programme is a fusion of socialist and ecological demands. It stands for the interests of the working class in society and in running the state. It advocates measures against pollution of the environment and the replacement of fossil fuels by renewable energy resources. It believes that inherent in capitalism's quest for profits is the harm it causes nature. Its slogans are 'red must be green and green must be red'. (Traub and Conway 2009)

ECOSOCIALIST ASIA

In mainland China, academics teach courses under the title 'ecosocialism' and discuss its merits. One of the highest-ranking Chinese environmentalists is Pan Yue, deputy director of China's State Environmental Protection Administration (SEPA). He has argued that while neither he nor the Chinese government endorses ecosocialism, they are interested in how it can influence their approach to the environment. However, China's swift economic growth and openness to large corporations makes it difficult to achieve environmental protection. Yue has been frank about the costs of growth in China:

> China's environmental crisis has arisen, basically, because our mode of economic modernization has been copied from western, developed nations.
>
> In 20 years, China has achieved economic results that took a century to attain in the west. But we have also concentrated a century's worth of environmental issues into those 20 years. While becoming the world leader in GDP growth and foreign investment, we have also become the world's number one consumer of coal, oil

and steel – and the largest producer of CO_2 and chemical oxygen demand (COD) emissions.

With the rise of globalization, developed countries have transferred their industry to developing nations as a form of environmental colonialism. In China, pollution has been moved from east to west and from the city to the rural areas. The rich consume and the poor suffer the pollution. The economic and environmental inequalities caused by a flawed understanding of growth and political achievement, held by some officials, have gone against the basic aims of socialism and abandoned the achievements of Chinese socialism. (Pan 2007)

Environmental protest in China has grown rapidly. In 2008, blogs and mass texts were used to mobilise protest against a $5.5 billion ethylene plant under construction by PetroChina in Chengdu. Protesters avoided the need for official permission by arguing they were just going for a stroll; four hundred people took part in the protest stroll:

'We're not dissidents,' said Wen Di, an independent blogger and former journalist living in Chengdu. 'We're just people who care about our homeland. What we're saying is that if you want to have this project, you need to follow certain procedures: for example, a public hearing and independent environmental assessment. We want a fair and open process.' (Wong 2008)

In 2009, a petro-chemical works was moved in Guangzhou after environmental protests (Mitchell 2009).

In the Philippines, the Revolutionary Workers Party-Mindanao, which left the New Communist Party, is a strong advocate of ecosocialist politics. British ecosocialist and Fourth International member Alan Thornett noted:

Most impressive from a practical point of view was the Philippines section – the Revolutionary Workers Party-Mindanao. They not only talked about the impact of extreme weather events on the region caused by climate change but how they are seeking to create sustainable agriculture in the Chiapas-type zone they control. They are, for example, replacing Monsanto modified rice, which has had its power to germinate as seed destroyed, with traditional rice strains which the farmers can use as seed. (Thornett 2010)

In India, there are massive ecological struggles as indigenous people once again are under assault, with their land being confiscated for mining and timber. In East India, a largely forgotten war is taking place between Maoist guerrillas and the indigenous against the Indian military. However, if successful, the Maoists may, as in China, seek to create capitalist industrialisation, and have had a brutal record in many parts of the world, including Peru and most notoriously Cambodia. Those more sympathetic to the Maoists argue that in Nepal they have supported democracy and are the only real allies that most indigenous people have. The novelist Arundhati Roy, who wrote *The God of Small Things*, reported on the conflict:

The antagonists in the forest are disparate and unequal in almost every way. On one side is a massive paramilitary force armed with the money, the firepower, the media, and the hubris of an emerging Superpower. On the other, ordinary villagers armed with traditional weapons, backed by a superbly organised, hugely motivated Maoist guerrilla fighting force with an extraordinary and violent history of armed rebellion. The Maoists and the paramilitary are old adversaries and have fought older avatars of each other several times before: Telangana in the '50s; West Bengal, Bihar, Srikakulam in Andhra Pradesh in the late '60s and '70s; and then again in Andhra Pradesh, Bihar and Maharashtra from the '80s all the way through to the present. They are familiar with each other's tactics, and have studied each other's combat manuals closely. Each time, it seemed as though the Maoists (or their previous avatars) had been not just defeated, but literally, physically exterminated. Each time, they have re-emerged, more organised, more determined and more influential than ever. Today once again the insurrection has spread through the mineral-rich forests of Chhattisgarh, Jharkhand, Orissa and West Bengal – homeland to millions of India's tribal people, dreamland to the corporate world.

It's easier on the liberal conscience to believe that the war in the forests is a war between the Government of India and the Maoists, who call elections a sham, Parliament a pigsty and have openly declared their intention to overthrow the Indian State. It's convenient to forget that tribal people in Central India have a history of resistance that predates Mao by centuries. (That's a truism of course. If they didn't, they wouldn't exist.) The Ho, the Oraon, the Kols, the Santhals, the Mundas and the Gonds have all rebelled several times, against the British, against zamindars and moneylenders. The rebellions were cruelly crushed, many thousands killed, but the people were never conquered. Even after Independence, tribal people were at the heart of the first uprising that could be described as Maoist, in Naxalbari village in West Bengal (where the word Naxalite – now used inter-changeably with 'Maoist' – originates). (Roy 2010)

Ecofeminism is also represented in India by intellectuals and activists such as Vandana Shiva and, of course, Arundhati Roy. The land conflicts in India involve millions of people at the grassroots, often drawing on ancient traditions of ecological concern. To some extent, Gandhi created an ecosocialist legacy and there are even green religious traditions such as that of the Bishnois (www.bishnoism.com); however, there is no formal ecosocialist network in India at present and plans for a Green Party are at an early stage.

A RED-GREEN EUROPE

Today, ecosocialism is a patchwork of different groups, networks and political parties. In Britain, the Fourth International's Socialist Resistance has embraced ecosocialism, arguing that given the unecological nature of much twentieth-century socialism and the urgency of climate change, the term 'ecosocialism' is of great importance. There is a strong ecosocialist group in the Green Party of England and Wales, Green Left, and an independent ecosocialist party, the Alliance for Green Socialism.

Sections of the Fourth International are committed to ecosocialism in many countries; for example, the SAP/LCR in Belgium is strongly ecosocialist. Green parties in Portugal, parts of Spain and Italy are explicitly ecosocialist. In Holland, four existing political parties, including the Communist Party, merged to create the Green Left in 1989. This Dutch Green Left Party is now very much part of the mainstream European Green Party.

A range of green socialist political parties exists, with a great deal of variation in their origins, outlook and policies. Greens and left parties have formed part of the broad opposition to the right in Italy, where the situation in the country is complex, fluid and divided on regional lines. In 2010, the green left has made gains in some regions, according to ecosocialist activist Fabio Barteri from Ecorise:

In 2005 a brand new candidate of the far left, Nicola Vendola, had won the primary elections for presidential run in Apulia, in the centre-left coalition. Young, communist and homosexual. He represented a real novelty and we still consider him the 'Italian Obama'. He won the elections by proposing a strong ecologist and socialist policy during his term. His party, Sinistra Ecologia e Libertà (Left, Ecology and Freedom) reached the 10% in Apulia. (Wall 2010)

Ecorise is described as an 'ecosocialist political laboratory':

> We are all students of biology, environmental and natural science, geology and engineering who want to bring the ecological issues back to the political debate in the University Movement and public opinion.
>
> Our aim is to produce independent information based on a website, an independent web-tv, a monthly newspaper (500 copies), a facebook page, meetings and conferences and even flash mobs.
>
> In Italy it is very hard to set up political groups because of the heterogeneity of the political views. In fact, we have five communist parties, two green parties, two social democrat parties and a lot of independent and anarchist groups. The left is divided. In Ecorise we have been able to gather a lot of different political views. (Barteri 2010)

'The Left', a new ecosocialist party in Switzerland, was launched in 2009, consisting of three already existing left parties; an ecosocialist network has recently been established in Turkey. The Left Bloc in Portugal have also embraced ecosocialism, while red-green politics are strongest perhaps in Scandinavia.

THE NORDIC GREEN LEFT

The Nordic Green Left is a coordination of Communist Parties and red-green parties who sit together in the European Parliament. In Scandinavia, traditional left parties and trade unions have become sympathetic to ecological politics.

In Norway, a red-green coalition – of the Labour Party, the Socialist Left Party and the Centre Party – won the

2005 election. The Socialist Left Party was created by a merger of the Communist Party of Norway and two other left parties in 1975; it claims radical credentials, quoting Brecht and embracing red and green in its party colours (SV Sentralt 2008). However, Norway still continues to be highly dependent on oil for its wealth and, despite a green-tinged government, supports whaling.

In 2009, after 18 years of neo-liberal government, a green-left coalition won power in Iceland, with the Socialist Alliance on 27 per cent and the Green Left Movement on 21 per cent. The Green Left have gained at the expenses of the right-wing free market parties because of their proud record of pointing out the risks of failing to regulate the banks and reliance on finance capital. The Green Left and the Socialists are keen to diversify the Icelandic economy and to make sure that finance capital is no longer king. Both ruling parties believe in raising income tax on higher earners and are pledged to preserve workers' rights and the Icelandic welfare state. The victory has also delivered the world's first openly lesbian prime minister.

The Green Left are hostile to NATO and are keen to maintain a demilitarised Iceland. The coalition government faces a number of big challenges. For example, the Socialists are keen to fast-track Iceland into the European Union, while the Green Left are, in contrast, eurosceptics who see the EU as a capitalist club. All parties are worried that Iceland's reputation as the most sustainable fishing nation in Europe, with relatively successful policies to conserve cod, could be destroyed by entry into the EU's common fisheries policy. The government continues to support whaling and the economic crisis has brought in the International Monetary Fund, a move far from green or left policies.

Jaap Krater from Saving Iceland, a coalition that has been taking non-violent action to protect the island, is sceptical:

> The left greens have not done as well as they hoped for. What has been more disappointing, they have supported putting public money into construction of a new Century Aluminum smelter just south of Reykjavik, because Century had difficulty financing the project. It is also noticeable that one of the more vocal opponents of the aluminum industry, Kolbrún Halldórsdóttir, has been ousted. Perhaps she was too much of a genuine environmentalist. (Wall 2009a)

Margaret Wright, a Green Party International Committee member from Cambridge, England, has noted more optimistically:

> At a meeting with Ögmundur Jónasson, re-elected member of the Red/Green Group, I heard the classic case Greens make against EU membership – free trade, conventional economic growth, potential militarisation, centralisation and loss of regional autonomy. I also heard the priorities of the Red/Greens as they enter government. They included:
>
> - the upgrading and protection of the welfare state, which long years of rightwing rule have undermined;
> - protection of natural resources and the environment, ownership of Iceland's resources which are currently in danger of falling into other's hands;
> - a diversified economy, sustainability, democracy and gender equality;
> - military non-alignment with withdrawal from NATO. (Wall 2009a)

The government has so far managed to resist welfare cuts, defend asylum rights and introduce a number of new women-friendly policies. They are also keen advocates of open source and free information, quotas for women on company boards have been introduced and strip clubs made illegal. Iceland's energy is already 100 per cent renewable, based on geothermal power, so the country is low carbon.

Drifa Snaedal, secretary-general of the Left-Green Movement, roots the Icelandic crisis in a global move towards neo-liberalism:

> Politicians all over the world sold our property to friends and families, but mostly men did so with the urge to reign and keep the power over communities, people and counties. This is what happened in Iceland and in many other parts of the world. At bargain prices, governments sold away what was rightfully the people's common property. Power slipped from our hands, from the hands of rightfully elected women and men. In Iceland, a small society of only 300 thousand inhabitants, we saw great power move into the hands of about 30 young businessmen. These were men a little older than I am now, with big egos and high ideas for a small island, but mostly for themselves.

She also argues that:

> Our main task in the coming years is to steer Icelandic society through the depression without privatizing our welfare system or our educational system. We must come through, without having to sell our resources to greedy multinational corporations. These corporations watch every step we take with the look of predators in their eye, wanting to make money off our difficulties. We will not manage to protect our society against these dangers, if we are not guided by the gender perspective. (Vinstri Græn 2010)

AUSTRALIA

Australia has been an important country for ecosocialist thought and action. In the 1970s, the 'green ban' movement emerged, led by Jack Mundey of the Builders Workers Union. His union refused to construct buildings that damaged conservation zones. Drawing upon both the insights of the Frankfurt School and the actions of the Australian green trade unionists like Mundey, the physicist Alan Roberts wrote *The Self-Managing Environment* (1979). Today, this remains one of the best books on ecosocialism, looking at the links between capitalism and environmental destruction, showing how a lack of democracy and workplace alienation fuel consumerism. Roberts also identified Marx's notion of the metabolism between humanity and the rest of nature, examined how capitalism distorts technological development, and showed how the commons was a source of ecological solutions, not a problem to be privatised. Roberts is also interesting because his origins were within Australian Trotskyism: he and his comrade Nick Origlass were extremely important in the development of ecosocialism. They saw environmental politics as absolutely vital but, more than this, they were activists and organized politically. Origlass was expelled from the Labour Party for opposing a waste dump in a working-class community, and he used non-violent direct action, elections (he was elected and re-elected as a local councillor) and trade union action to promote ecosocialist struggles (Greenland 1998). Both Roberts and Origlass have seen ecology as a socialist issue that impacts on working-class communities.

Democratic Socialist Perspective (DSP) is active in the Australian Socialist Alliance and publishes *Green Left Weekly*, which promotes ecosocialism. Rather than being a group that has moved from red to green, the DSP sees ecosocialism as an essential form of politics that must be built to tackle the multiple environmental and social crises on this planet.

New Zealand, which has a strong and radical Green Party with a number of Members of Parliament, has also seen recent calls for the creation of an ecosocialist network.

NORTH AMERICA

In the US, there are a number of ecosocialists active in the Greens or in socialist organisations. The US also has indigenous activists who advocate ecological politics. John Bellamy Foster's impressive work on the links between Marxism and ecology can be situated in the tradition of the journal *Monthly Review*, of which Foster is editor. The journal was established in the 1940s and pioneered a Marxist politics that was open, innovative and democratic, rejecting a party line and developing new ideas. Its founder Paul Sweezy wrote extensively on ecosocialist themes in the 1970s with essays on 'socialism and ecology' and a Marxist analysis of the car culture. It would be difficult to review all of the varied US contributors to the development of ecosocialism, but it is important to mention Professor Barry Commoner. A biology professor, Commoner was one of the most high-profile figures in the environmental movement in the late 1960s and 1970s as well as a committed socialist. He challenged the Malthusian ecologists like Paul Ehrlich, arguing that technological choices rather than population was the key factor determining environmental damage (Commoner 1971). Commoner, of course, was representative of a wider tradition of socialist natural scientists. With the financial support of the German Greens, he established the Citizens Party and ran for US president in 1980.

The Citizens Party was eventually dissolved, but many of its members went on to be active in the Green Party. Prominent ecosocialists in the US Green Party have included the late Walt Sheasby and the late Peter Camajeo. The development of Green Party politics in the US has been particularly complex and I am unable here to develop much detail. For example, there were for a while two different Green Party networks, one rather more decentralist and the other rather more formal. The relationship between the campaigner Ralph Nader and the Greens has been another source of complexity.

In Canada, the Green Party moved to the right during the 1990s, under the leadership of pro-business leader and ex-Conservative Jim Harris. In response, a number of ex-Green Party members formed a Peace and Ecology Party, but this did not take off. Elizabeth May's election as a new leader, has encouraged some on the left to rejoin. An ecosocialist, Dan Murray, was recently elected to the Canadian Green Party executive after standing on an ecosocialist platform.

Socialist Voice is a network that strongly promotes ecosocialist politics in Canada, and I am inspired by their positive work on green politics, socialism and indigenous issues. There are also very strong and militant indigenous groups, many of whom have links with indigenous activists fighting for the environment in Latin America.

Increasingly, grassroots movements for environmental justice, while rarely using the title 'ecosocialist', are mobilising for the ecosocialist values of environmental protection, radical democracy, and land and social justice. These movements are often huge in China and India; for example, there have been protests against big dams that have displaced or threaten to displace communities, involving hundreds of thousands of people. In Europe, radical ecologists have used non-violent direct action to challenge both climate change and the capitalist logic that fuels it. In Britain, for example, Climate Camp, which has evolved from the anti-roads campaign Reclaim the Streets (RTS), mobilises many thousands of individuals to use direct action against environmental destruction. RTS targeted the financial centre of London in an action on 19 June 1999 and disrupted it with an occupation involving 7,000 people. In the twenty-first century, militant environmental direct action is growing with an emphasis on anti-capitalist ideas. Organisers of the Dutch-Belgian climate camp, which was inspired by the British example, argue that 'the climate crisis is one of the symptoms of a failing capitalist system, and the most urgent crisis that makes a drastic change of course of our society necessary' (Klimaat Actie Kamp 2009, author's translation).

Indigenous communities are becoming increasingly well organised and politically active internationally. From Canada to Papua New Guinea and from Peru to Australia, indigenous networks have fought against the enclosure of their land, for radical environmental demands and social justice. In Greenland, an ecosocialist indigenous party took power in 2009. The indigenous movements are strongest in Latin America and the success of the left in Latin America at the beginning of the twenty-first century has been partly a product of their dynamism.

In Europe, North America and Australia, ecosocialism is normally thought of as a product of thinkers such as Marx and Engels (essentially, of white Europeans); however, at present, ecosocialism is undoubtedly strongest in Latin America. The success of ecosocialism in Latin America is discussed in greater detail in Chapter 5.

5
Ecosocialism in Latin America

A member of his community, he tells us, conducted some Swedish tourists to a Quechua village near Cuzco. Impressed by the collectivist spirit of the indigenous community, one of the tourists commented: 'This is like communism.'

'No', responded their guide, 'Communism is like this.'

Hugo Blanco, quoted in Riddell 2008

The Bolivarian revolution is an important support for the salvation of humanity, and also the salvation of nature.

Both entities are closely related, human and nature, because humans are part of nature and nature is part of humanity.

Therefore, for the developed world, as you may call it, this current level of development of the countries of the North, of Australia, of Europe, must be made sustainable. Therefore, socialism is [necessary for] the salvation of the entire world.

Hugo Chavez, quoted in McIlroy 2009

5. Indigenous activists marching in Ecuador (Donovan & Scott)

PERU

On 5 June 2009, World Environment Day, President Alan
Garcia sent the police, a heavily armed militia, to break up
an indigenous blockade at Bagua, in the rainforest province
of Amazonas in Peru. The indigenous people were fired on
by police and many were killed. They were taking part in the
largest uprising of Peruvian indigenous people since the Tupac
revolt of 1781. Garcia's government had sought to relax legal
restrictions so that oil corporations could take indigenous
land in the rainforests. After centuries of exploitation, the
Peruvian indigenous people of the Amazon had decided that
they must resist the destruction of their society; time after
time, despite promises to the contrary, their land had been

seized and they had been forced into poverty. In 2008 and again in 2009, indigenous people had blockaded roads, cut off energy supplies and paralysed river transport in their attempts to hold on to their land. They have enjoyed a high level of support from Peruvians living outside the rainforests. In June 2009, workers went on strike in solidarity with the indigenous, and non-indigenous Peruvians have protested throughout the country.

Despite severe repression, the indigenous people won their fight in 2008 and 2009, forcing the Peruvian Congress to repeal the laws that threatened their land. Even so, this has been at some cost in terms of loss of life, imprisonment and injury. The indigenous leader Alberto Pizango sought shelter in the Nicaraguan Embassy and as I write, remains in exile. All across Latin America, similar stories of indigenous people using protest to protect their land can be found as they become increasingly well organized. In Latin America, though not yet in Peru, left governments have come to power. Both the indigenous protests and left electoral victories are part of a complex and sometimes contradictory trend in Latin American politics. More than in any other region of the world, demands for social justice, ecological politics and radical democracy are leading to political change.

As a long-standing Peruvian socialist, Hugo Blanco was radicalised in a green direction by spending time with the Zapatistas in Mexico. In 1994, the Zapatistas revolted against the North American Free Trade Area (NAFTA) agreement, which united Mexico, Canada and the US in neo-liberal economic policies; the Zapatistas' actions contributed to a process of transformation which is currently sweeping the region. Indigenous activism is increasingly shaping the

Latin American left, with an emphasis on ecology, justice and defence of the commons.

The indigenous struggle has continued on the continent for over five hundred years. The destruction of American indigenous communities began in 1492, with the arrival of Columbus in Cuba in the Caribbean. He landed in the Bahamas, and met local people who showered his crew members with gifts. Obsessed with finding gold to pay for his trip, Columbus and his crew resorted to killing indigenous people if they did not provide him with the metal. As a result of European colonialism in the Americas, millions of indigenous people died in a genocide, through slavery, slaughter and disease. The conquest of the Americas was inspired by the drive to extract resources as quickly as possible and laid the basis along with African slavery for the development of capitalism in Western Europe. The devastation of humanity and the rest of nature has been huge. Latin American countries in the twentieth century were generally ruled by and for the benefit of an elite minority of largely European descendents. Despite centuries of revolt, by 1990, Latin America was run on largely free market neo-liberal policies. Even those on the left argued that a revolt against the IMF, WTO and the multinationals was impossible (Castañeda 1993).

VENEZUELA

Since the late 1990s, Latin America has moved to the left. In 1998, Hugo Chavez was elected as Venezuelan president; he survived a coup attempt in 2002 and was re-elected in 2006. Chavez has become the most influential socialist leader in the world and is sympathetic to much of the ecosocialist vision. In Brazil, though he has often disappointed the left, and his government has been marred by corruption scandals, the election and re-election of Worker Party leader Lula in 2002 and 2006, has also been significant. In Ecuador, after huge social movement mobilisations, Rafael Correa, an ally of Chavez was elected in 2006 and re-elected in 2009. Evo Morales, the Latin American leader most explicitly advocating ecosocialism, was elected president of Bolivia in 2005. Perhaps most remarkable of all has been the transformation of the politics of Paraguay, a country which had been ruled for 34 years by right-wing dictator Alfredo Stroessner, followed by nearly 20 years of largely right-wing party rule: in 2008, a former Catholic archbishop, Fernando Lugo, was elected leader on a platform committed to the poor and the indigenous. In Uruguay, a coalition of left parties, the Frente Amplio ('Broad Front'), are currently in power, having won the presidency and a majority of congress seats in 2004 and in 2009. A major dispute has continued between Uruguay and its neighbour Argentina, over a planned paper plant which opponents argue would create severe pollution in Uruguay. In Chile and Argentina, centre-left candidates have also won office, displacing the right. In El Salvador, the former guerrillas of the FLM were elected into office in 2009 and the Sandinistas regained power in neighbouring Nicaragua.

The Zapatistas, named after the Mexican revolutionary leader Emiliano Zapata, rose up in January 1994 in protest at the creation of the North American Free Trade Area. They believed this agreement between Mexico, the US and Canada would lead to land being seized from indigenous people. The Zapatistas, who originated in the Chiapas region of Mexico on the border with Guatemala, have rejected Leninist concepts of revolution and draw upon anarchist, indigenous and even

Christian religious inspiration, as well as Marxism. They seized land which was occupied by absentee landlords and created autonomous communities right across the region. Zapatistas utilised the Internet to spread their ideas and, building an international network, they brought together anti-capitalist movements, such as the Reclaim the Streets network in Britain, from across the world to create a global form of protest. In June 1999, a Zapatista-inspired global day of action against capitalism created a wave of protest across the world, including an occupation of Britain's financial centre in the city of London by 5,000 activists. The Zapatistas have never used the term 'ecosocialist', but adhere to the key assumptions of the ecosocialist movement. Launching a rebellion during Latin America's so-called 'lost decade', when the whole region was dominated by US interests and right-wing governments, the Zapatistas were a key ingredient in the wider changes that have spread through the region.

Hugo Chavez has proved to be the most radical elected head of state in the region and has provided leadership that is influencing all of Latin America and beyond. A former army education officer, he took part in a military uprising after the Venezuelan government had killed rioters protesting an IMF austerity programme. Elected in 1999, he has steadily moved to the left ever since. Initially seeking a 'third way' between right and left, he has been radicalised by the opposition of the wealthy Venezuelan elite to his government. He was removed by right-wing coup in 2002, but swiftly returned to power. He has worked closely with the Cuban government and has sought to build socialism in Venezuela under the slogan 'Venezuela Ahora es de Todos': 'Today Venezuela is for everyone.' He has invested oil revenue in health care, education and anti-poverty programmes (Wilpert 2007).

Eva Golinger has asked, 'Did anyone from Greenpeace or Earth First! ever imagine that the world's first environmental president would come from Venezuela?' (Golinger 2007). Despite being highly dependent on oil revenue, Chavez has made numerous statements endorsing an ecosocialist approach. Visiting London in 2006, he spoke out against universal car ownership, 'One car each? Our planet won't stand that – that model of capitalism, extreme individualism and consumerist egotism. The destructive so-called developmentalism destroying the planet is, quite frankly, a thing of stupidity – una cosa de tontos', before telling an audience which included London Mayor Ken Livingstone that if the entire population of the planet consumed like the average American five planet Earths would be needed.

Caracas, the capital city of Venezuela, is badly polluted by car fumes; petrol is cheaper than bottled water in this oil-rich state. However, Chavez has made major efforts to green the country. A new metro line was built and commuters rode for free for the first six months, to reduce car use. A joint venture to build bicycles with Iran has been launched. Organic agriculture is heavily promoted, incorporating permaculture principles. Tree-planting projects, 'Mission Arbol', are important. Controversial gold- and coal-mining projects have been closed to protect the environment and indigenous people. The environment ministry has a strong influence over policy members and ecosocialists are active at a governmental level. Revenue from oil is being invested in renewable energy in Venezuela.

Chavez is extremely keen to develop commons-based property rights to increase living standards, while improving management of the environment. Typically, water councils bring water users together to create sustainable supplies.

Venezuela is promoting a new kind of development model: agrarian reform, cooperative enterprise, organic agriculture, use of local resources – these are all features of an entirely new socioeconomic model for Venezuela. The model is summed up in a programme called the 'Vuelvan Caras' Mission (a term almost impossible to translate), which attempts to coordinate all the other programmes and missions: it provides government assistance in the form of technical advice and funds derived from oil income, for agricultural, industrial and commercial cooperatives, generating employment and training. It encourages local initiative, self-sufficiency, sustainability and 'endogenous development', development from within and from below, with popular participation. The leading role of women, blacks and indigenous people is also explicitly promoted. This new model will take years to develop, but it is already under way and being promoted with great enthusiasm (Raby 2004).

Venezuela is no panacea: despite good intentions, Caracas remains highly polluted and the entire economy is very dependent on petroleum exports. However, it is actively attempting to move towards a greener society and is strongly supportive of positive social change throughout Latin America. Finally, it is explicitly socialist but seeks to construct a participatory form of socialism.

BOLIVIA

In Bolivia, the indigenous leader Evo Morales was elected president in 2005. Like Venezuela, Bolivia is polarised between an elite who look to North America and the poorer majority. Decades of struggles against water privatisation and other neo-liberal measures has led to the growth of strong social movements based on the indigenous. Morales has changed the constitution, giving indigenous people new rights that guarantee participation. He is also known for his ecosocialist commitments, challenging capitalism because of the damage it does to the environment. He also argues that defence of Pachamama, Mother Earth, is central to the indigenous vision. He has been virtually the only national leader to call for a zero-carbon economy. In April 2009, he told the UN 'we don't own the planet [but rather] we belong to it', arguing that 'Mother Earth cannot be a piece of merchandise.'

In a speech given in November 2008, he argued, 'Climate change has placed before all humankind a great choice: to continue in the ways of capitalism and death, or to start down the path of harmony with nature and respect for life', before adding 'The Earth is much more important than the stock exchanges of Wall Street and the world.'

CUBA

Cuba has introduced some of the most radical ecological reforms in the world. The permaculture model in Cuba has been accompanied by investment in renewable energy and public transport. Strong conservation laws have been introduced to protect wildlife. While the greening of Cuba was fuelled by necessity, as cheap oil was removed from the economy by the collapse of the Soviet Union, both the actions of the Nature and Humanity Foundation, an independent environmental NGO, and former president Fidel Castro's environmental concerns have led to changes.

Both Cuba and Venezuela have given practical support to neighbouring countries who have sought to reduce their CO_2 emissions; for example, Cuba has helped Jamaica introduce low-energy light bulbs.

ECUADOR

In Ecuador, Rafael Correa, an ally of Morales and Chavez, was elected with the support of the social movements and indigenous people. The constitution of Ecuador has enshrined ecological protection. The land rights of indigenous people have been strengthened and the government has supported court action against the US oil company Chevron to compensate indigenous people for damage to their land. Correa has also introduced policies for wildlife conservation, including shark protection. Ecuador is yet another oil-dependent economy, but Correa has sought to halt oil exploration in the Ecuadorian rainforest in return for international finance. However, Correa, despite these measures and much support from indigenous people, has also been critical of indigenous people who have sought to prevent oil and mineral extraction. In 2009, Correa's government attacked indigenous and environmental protests at mining. In February 2010, an oil minister critical of drilling in the Amazon was sacked and attempts were made to close an indigenous radio station.

Correa is a good illustration of the environmental contradictions of Latin American left governments. Correa is a Washington-trained economist and is less radical than Chavez and Morales; however, at root, the problem is structural rather than personal. While the new and radical Latin American left leaders are critical of traditional development models that focus on swift industrialisation, concerned with environmental damage and seeking to represent indigenous and black citizens excluded from participation, countries such as Bolivia, Venezuela and Ecuador are highly dependent on resource extraction. Without oil in Venezuela and Ecuador or natural gas in Bolivia, such countries would have little to export. There is clearly a paradox, when it comes to introducing ecosocialist policies. It is extremely important to recognise the huge gains made by these countries. It is also interesting to note that while the German Greens and other European green parties failed to march through the state on behalf of the social movement and instead were to a large extent incorporated into existing structures, the Latin American left have made major and impressive structural changes. None the less, the cutting edge of ecosocialist ideas and politics comes from grassroots organisations rather than the state.

BRAZIL

An excellent illustration of ecosocialism emerging from the grassroots is the recent experience of Brazil. After decades of military dictatorship, former steel worker Lula da Silva was elected Brazil's president as a member of the Workers Party (PT). Committed to social justice and ecological reforms, the Workers Party was seen as representing radical democracy, in the form of participatory budgets. Unusually for Latin America, Brazil has a Green Party, which has participated in the PT coalition government. Brazil also has a strong Ecosocialist Network and a history of radical green activism. During the 1980s, the rubber tapper Chico Mendes fought against the landowners who sought to destroy the rainforests of the Amazon; the landowners murdered Mendes, triggering a global outcry. However, da Silva, elected after Venezuela's Chavez, was in a far weaker position than more recently elected left leaders on the continent. Relatively isolated internationally when he was first elected, his party have had to compromise to gain the support of right-wing parties in order to remain in government and receive support for legislation. The demands of the IMF have reduced radicalism and the PT government has been badly affected by corruption scandals. Marina Silva, a committed ecosocialist, was appointed environment minister and worked hard to defend the Amazon and its people. She was a close friend of Mendes and like him was a member of a rubber-tapper community, which had a commitment to protecting the forests that gave them a livelihood extracting rubber from trees. However, Silva lacked cabinet allies, and the government, although introducing some measures to protect the Amazon, saw the demands of indigenous people and environmentalists as standing in the way of economic growth and accumulation. Exhausted and marginalised, Silva resigned as environment minister in 2008.

Brazil has sought to expand biofuels, to flood forests to create hydroelectricity, and to introduce genetically modified crops. Silva believes she made gains as a minister but she also suffered major defeats:

She talks of an environmental awakening in Brazil and around the world, 'a new political pact with society that wants Brazil to develop but with the preservation of the Amazon, the Atlantic rainforest, the savannah and of all our water reserves'. She is also adamant that this engagement has enabled a crackdown on the illegal loggers.

'Without the support of society it would have been impossible to have put 600 people involved in environmental crimes in the Amazon in jail,' she says. 'This is something that is achieved by a new social pact that is appearing inside and outside of the country.'

While supporters have described her exit from power as a defeat for the green cause, she insists that progress is being made. 'Twenty years ago, there were politicians who promised chainsaws to their voters to win elections ... Now we have a resolution that says neither public nor private banks can fund projects in an area that is being illegally deforested.' (Phillips 2008)

Marina was replaced as minister by a member of the Brazilian Green Party. Critics argue that the Greens are dominated by career politicians with little real interest in the environment; however, in yet another twist, Marina Silva confirmed in 2009 she would run for president as a Green Party candidate.

There are huge and militant social movements in Brazil that support ecosocialist goals. Diverse indigenous communities also fight for land and against logging, ranching and big dams that flood land. As in other parts of Latin America, these communities are increasingly active and have won some victories. The Landless Movement (MST) occupies unused land that has been monopolised by the elites. It is critical of the export monoculture model, noting that Lula has pursued the same policies as early right-wing governments. The government gives priority to monocultures destined for export, under the control of transnational companies and foreign financial capital, to sustain the neo-liberal economic policies inherited from President Fernando Henrique Cardoso. Instead, MST argues for 'an agro-ecological production network and aimed at promoting food sovereignty, with the agro-industrial priority of cooperative farming and of guaranteed education for settlers at all levels (see <http://www.mstbrazil.org/>). The MST have carried out huge land occupations involving hundreds of thousands of people. However, they have also faced repression, with many of their number being killed by thugs employed by landowners.

PARAGUAY, CHILE, ARGENTINA

The La Soja Mata (which means 'Soya kills') network works in Brazil and neighbouring countries such as Paraguay, against agricultural monocultures dependent on pesticides. Such monocultures take land from smallholding peasants and indigenous people, are highly oil dependent, and use deadly toxins. The campaign around the death of 11-year-old Silvino Tavera in Paraguay illustrates the stakes of their campaign. In 2003, Silvino was accidentally sprayed with a fungicide and died a few days later (La Soja Mata 2006). Other members of his family and the local community were hospitalised. However, despite an attempt at prosecution, the soya producers who had sprayed indiscriminately were freed from jail after a campaign by soya companies. Local thugs were bribed to attack Tavera's family when they continued to campaign for justice. Eighty per cent of soya in Paraguay comes from genetically modified crops, which are very dependent on toxic pesticides.

For decades, peasants have been bullied into selling their land and land-ownership patterns in Paraguay are probably the most unequal in the whole of South America. After decades of one-party rule, much of it under the dictator Stroessner, one of the most remarkable left victories occurred in 2008, when Fernando Lugo, a former Catholic archbishop, was elected president. In a country with such a strong elite, Lugo's progress in creating change is likely to be slow, but his victory has allowed some space for peasants, workers and the indigenous to organise politically and fight back.

In 1973, Chile's socialist government under President Allende was overthrown in a violent coup, supported by the US. The right tortured its opponents and murdered many thousands on the left. The coup leader Pinochet was not defeated until 1989. Since then, there have been five democratic elections. In the fifth, in 2010, Chile elected a right-wing presidential candidate, Sebastián Piñera, who defeated the centre-left candidate.

Chile is dependent on copper exports and there is conflict with the largest group of indigenous people, the Mapuche. There are 600,000 people in Chile who identify themselves as Mapuche (the people of the earth), and they are currently battling for the restoration of lost land rights. The Mapuche have a long history of struggle: in 1641, they defeated the Spanish and agreed a treaty maintaining their land. Later centuries saw the erosion of these rights and their land. The socialist government of Allende restored those rights and land to some extent. However, with the assassination of Allende and Auguste Pinochet's violent coup, the gains of the Mapuche were reversed. In the third millennium, they are once again in conflict and 15 Mapuche political prisoners are currently in jail in Chile.

Much of the land claimed by the Mapuche is made up of ecologically important temperate forests; however, the forests have been logged in many places and replaced by monocultures of eucalyptus and other non-native trees. The destruction of the forest has reduced biodiversity and disrupted water supplies. Maria Theresa Panchillo, a Mapuche environmental activist notes: 'The Mapuche people believe that we are the guardians of our magical forests … When we fight to save these forests, we are also fighting for our way of life that depends upon these forests' (Wilson 2003).

Marco Enríquez-Ominami, an independent candidate backed by Greens and the left, contested Chile's recent presidential election; he is the son of the leader of the Revolutionary Left

Movement, Miguel Enríquez, who was killed in the 1973 coup. Due to disillusionment with the Concertación coalition of left and right, Marco gained strength through running an imaginative blog-based campaign and came third in the first round of the election with 20 per cent. He resigned from the Socialist Party because he felt, like many other citizens, that the Concertación concentrated power in the hands of an elite few. He was endorsed by the small Chilean Green Party and campaigned strongly on environmental themes. He was also the first major presidential candidate in recent Chilean elections to seek to promote indigenous causes, and issued campaign material in the Mapuche language and expressed belief in constitutional change that would recognise the indigenous roots of the country. He has also campaigned strongly against environmentally damaging big dam projects and mining. However, Alfredo Seguel, a Mapuche activist and publisher of *Informativo Mapuexpress*, is sceptical: 'Some of the proposals put forward by Enríquez-Ominami on economic and environmental issues are very weak, including some that have a strong air of neoliberalism' (Tockman 2009). Many on the left, including ecosocialists, supported instead the candidacy of Jorge Arrate, a former minister in Allende's government, who is committed to building a pluralist left in Chile; Arrate gained 6 per cent. Both left candidates were eliminated in the first round in 2009, Piñera, the right-wing candidate, was elected with 51 per cent in 2010.

In Argentina, Mapuche and other indigenous people face racism, marginalisation and land seizures. Assaults on their way of life have been largely ignored by governments, whether authoritarian or more democratic. In recent decades, indigenous land has been taken for cattle ranching, forests have been clear-cut for paper, and the Pilcomayo River has been badly polluted with heavy metals. The left have gained some strength in Argentina, and the country has been allied with other states in Latin America with socialist governments. The financial collapse of Argentina in 1999 led to dynamic grassroots protest movements and an exciting factory occupation movement.

There are also a number of environmental organisations, but policies or programmes for ecosocialist goals seem rather more distant than in most Latin American states. The gains of indigenous people in neighbouring countries have given the indigenous people of Argentina some encouragement to organise. A recent ecosocialist network in Argentina, Marxismo Ecológico, is making some progress.

Ecosocialism has some influence in a number of Latin American countries and, even in the most conservative areas, battles are being won. Perhaps the most encouraging development, despite serious repression, is in Peru. Here, indigenous people have built an impressive political organisation and have taken successful non-violent direct action to defend the rainforests. The indigenous have acted as the cutting edge of a process of radical social change across the continent. The success of the left in Latin America should be studied with care by those who want to achieve an ecological, socially just and democratic alternative globally. This moves us on to the most important question of all, the question of strategy: *how* do we struggle for ecosocialism when we struggle for ecosocialism?

6
Slow the Train!

'Another World is not only possible. She is on her
way. On a quiet day, I can hear her breathing.'
Arundhati Roy (quoted in Hopkins 2008: 213)

'Spartacus emerges as the most capital fellow in
the whole history of antiquity. A great general (no
Garibaldi he), of noble character, a real representative of the proletariat of ancient times.'
Karl Marx (Marx and Engels 1975: 265)

The situation is sobering. Climate change may already be
beyond the tipping points that will accelerate climate chaos.
Rising carbon dioxide emissions look likely to acidify the
world's oceans and destroy marine food chains. There are
a range of other severe ecological problems. Inequality is
increasing and resource shortages look likely to fuel new
wars. The global stock of nuclear weapons is enough to kill
us all many times over. Michael Löwy has noted that in the
words of Walter Benjamin, revolutionary change is perhaps
'not the locomotive of history', but 'humanity reaching for
the emergency brakes of the train, before it goes down the
abyss' (Löwy 2009)

6. Indigenous protester injured by police at Bagua,
Peru (Thomas Quirynen)

We need to find realistic strategies for change and we need
to do so fast. The most important area of discussion for
ecosocialists must be 'how can we stop the train before it
leaps the rails?' The question of how ecosocialists fight for
change is the one we must ask and re-ask. Political strategy,
practical tactics, discussion of agency – that is, which social
groups are most motivated and resourced to create change

– are all of very great significance. Change will not occur automatically or easily.

Achieving change so as to avoid catastrophe can appear impossible. The scale of transformation necessary is daunting. It often appears as if every strategic avenue has been blocked. The maniacs who sustain a suicidal system seem to have persuaded, bribed, or otherwise incorporated radicals who have sought change through parliamentary politics. So often, the politics of taking state power, through building political parties, seeing them grow slowly and gradually gaining elected office, has failed. The political system has been better at changing radicals than radicals have been at changing the political system.

There are many examples: the German Greens moved from student opposition and the social movements against nuclear power and nuclear weapons to coalition government with the Social Democrats. The Greens introduced some positive reforms but they failed to transform the system and ending up supporting NATO as well as German military intervention abroad (Hockenos 2008). In Australia, Pete Garrett, the charismatic lead singer of rock band Midnight Oil, shifted from being a leading member of the Nuclear Disarmament Party in the 1980s to joining the Labor government of Australia as a Cabinet member in 2008. As Minister of the Environment, one of Garrett's most controversial acts was to give the go-ahead to a uranium mine, just the kind of mine that creates toxic pollution and fuels the nuclear weapons that he opposed for decades (ABC News 2009).

This is not a new process. In 1918, the internationalist and anti-war Socialist Parties did an almost instant about-turn and supported the military of their varied countries when the First World War broke out. The German Social Democrats supported the Kaiser's forces, the British Labour Party voted for armed intervention, the French Socialists endorsed war mobilisation, and so on. Parliamentary politicians look unlikely to pull the brake and stop the train. Indeed, much environmental reformism is about introducing policies that do not interfere with the acceleration, while making superficial changes that distract attention from the nature of the unfolding crisis.

If the road of gradual political reform seems blocked, the alternative of creating ever smaller and supposedly ideologically pure political organisations to the left of whatever else exists, also gives little hope. The far left in many countries is isolated from society, dividing over esoteric disputes and splintering with almost continuous motion.

There exists a kind of Leninist gnosticism, with the implicit assumption that if one digs far enough a secret formula for gaining power can be found which will deliver success. This produces a culture that can be highly destructive, leading to a misplaced search for certainty that alienates potential support and multiplies division. Leninist groups can wrongly assume that a tiny number of comrades armed with the correct theory can lead larger movements to victory. The gnosis, or secret knowledge, does not exist; there are no simple formulas for social transformation. Although this tendency to produce isolated and sectarian left groups is more pronounced in certain countries (Britain being one and Argentina another), it is almost universal, and while it is common amongst the Marxist far left, there are anarchist examples as well. Understandable despair at those who compromise can lead to political sterility. The ecosocialist Australian group Democratic Socialist Perspectives, trying to develop a less exclusive kind of politics has noted:

Small socialist organizations operating in relative isolation in the working class movements, or sometimes substantially outside these movements because they are composed almost totally of small groups of 'socialist intellectuals' are chronically plagued with what might be called 'Marxist' identity politics. That is they are more concerned about 'proving' to themselves that they are 'real Marxists' than actually applying what Marx, Engels and Lenin taught which is to build real socialist leadership in the working class. In fact, the further away such groups are from that objective, the more loudly they assert their 'Marxist' identity. What passes as politics in 'the left' as we have it in this country can degenerate to little more than a ridiculous I'm-more-Marxist-than-you pissing competition. We've all seen this time and again with various little sects. And we've also seen this tendency in our own organization. (Democratic Socialist Perspective 2009)

The DSP are interesting because such comments are to an extent self-criticism: the DSP used to be the Democratic Socialist Party but now see themselves as the Democratic Socialist Perspective within a much wider political landscape. The green anarchist Murray Bookchin, warned in his pamphlet 'Listen Marxist!'(in Bookchin 1971) of a sectarian politics, but time and time again, fought those who were close to his political and philosophical positions with frenzied aggression.

Another dead end has been to retreat into theory. Academic Marxism is a small industry and while Marxist academics have provided varied and important insights, academic work should not be entirely independent from practical politics. This to a large extent was the fate of elements of Western Marxism, especially the Frankfurt School. It is wrong to assume that the production of theory will lead to political change without political practice.

There is widespread disillusionment with political activity in many parts of the world; however, political change is undoubtedly needed to halt the forces of destruction. Lifestyle change is certainly not enough – as we have already noted, deeper structural transformation is necessary.

OUT OF THE TRAP

It would be easy, but inappropriate, to attack radicals who betray their politics, to dismiss the purist left, in its Leninist or anarchist forms, to decry academics who ignore practical struggle, or to ridicule those who believe small personal change can multiply to protect the biosphere. Such criticism would miss the point, which is that in a society where capitalism is so dominant and powerful, constructing a politics that will challenge it, will be almost impossibly difficult. False solutions will be attractive, when all solutions look likely to fail. Greens who sell out, dogmatists divided into political sects too fixated on ideological purity to act and academics that never leave their libraries, are all different faces of a common dilemma. It is not a dilemma that can be dogmatically or simply dealt with.

This chapter examines strategy and makes some suggestions; it does not claim to provide 'the answer'. However, if it encourages discussion which leads to focused and effective action, it will have achieved something. Despite the fact that thinking about political change can be daunting and it is easy to be pessimistic, it is possible to start to think about some forms of action that are likely to be effective.

Struggles over land rights and enclosure provide one starting-point for taking action to defend humanity and the rest of nature. As we have seen, the exploitation of the environment is often closely linked to social injustice and human rights abuse. There are thousands of examples of indigenous people, peasants and others being swept from their land, so that resources can be extracted to fuel profit. Very simply, being active to oppose such abuses provides an excellent starting-point for ecosocialist politics. In Bagua, the indigenous people were attacked and many of them killed while defending their land in the Peruvian rainforests. However, the indigenous people won: they were organised, and made links with communities right across Peru. The news of the massacre at Bagua was transmitted around the world by journalists and bloggers. Solidarity actions took place in Peru, including a strike by trade unionists, while in London, climate change activists blockaded the Peruvian Embassy. All of this solidarity work helped the indigenous people of the rainforests to resist the assault on their land by President Alan García's government.

The destruction of the rainforests will accelerate climate change, so they must be defended. The destruction of the rainforests to make way for oil and gas exploration will lead to even greater climate change, as more fossil fuels are burnt, heating the planet. As we have seen, much of the work which is said to be aimed at dealing with climate change may make it worse and is at best largely irrelevant. Stopping the destruction of ecosystems and preventing fossil-fuel extraction is an absolute priority. Such destruction can be fought. It is fought best on the ground by local people, but wherever we are on this planet, we can give solidarity. In Bagua, the indigenous network had organised support right across Peru, involving approximately fifty different ethnic indigenous groups in the campaign. Indigenous people from as far away as Canada went to Bagua to provide practical help. Hugo Blanco's *Lucha Indigena* ('Indigenous Struggle') newspaper, is one example of how struggles can be communicated across a whole region of the world, in this case, Latin America. Ecosocialists in Canada, Britain and Australia supported the struggle at Bagua.

However severe the environmental crisis becomes, the more fossil-fuel extraction can be slowed and the more biodiverse habitats can be maintained the better. Currently, environmental protection often ignores these vital insights – the success of indigenous people in maintaining ecosystems is almost totally forgotten by global environmental policy makers. The WTO, IMF and other neo-liberal institutions directly pursue policies that aim to enclose indigenous communal land; as we have noted, the present market-friendly climate change framework seeks to buy and sell the forest under the feet of those who live in them. Ecosocialists can work to encourage all environmentalists to make a priority all such struggles that directly protect nature. With a huge global environmental movement, the argument that environmentalists should directly support struggles to preserve diverse ecosystems is a persuasive one. Every battle won slows the train.

Often it is argued that given the urgency of climate change, it is inappropriate to wait 'for the revolution', or for radical solutions. I have been told on many occasions that to combine ecological and socialist demands is to delay the weaker reforms necessary to halt environmental destruction. Yet the ecosocialist struggles in defence of communities to control their resources in the face of corporate pressure for mining, oil extraction, biofuels, logging, and so on, are of immediate benefit if we are to halt climate change and other severe environmental threats.

Ecosocialism is the environmentalism not just of indigenous people, peasants and other communities who lived directly from the land, but of the poor. Relatively wealthy individuals have been able to displace environmental threats to those communities which are poorer. While the environmental crisis ultimately threatens all of us, the environmental crisis already kills and has been doing so for some time. The poorest are, literally, dumped on. For example, incinerators are most likely to be situated in African-American communities in the US, while motorways and chemical plants blight the landscapes of poorer communities. In South Africa, the anti-carbon trading activist Sajida Khan, worked to try and shut down a landfill dump next to her community. The Clean Development Mechanism kept the dump open by funding it in return for methane reduction. While methane reduction is a laudable aim, situating toxic dumps next to communities is not.

Sajida died of cancer in 2007. The dump was originally situated in a nature reserve during the apartheid era in 1980, but twenty-first-century climate policy kept it open and killed her (Bond and Dada 2007). Environmental racism is of course common, with minority communities being dumped upon and exploited.

RED HOT

Action on the ground against pollution which destroys lives is vital. Direct action can be used to fight incinerators, motorways and other manifestations of ecological destruction. An inspiring example of an ecosocialist who was at the forefront of such action was the late Nick Origlass. Nick, from Australia, was also a rare example of someone who took elected office without being corrupted and selling out, an individual involved in the thick of Marxist factionalism who could look further than the infighting; he was a working-class intellectual, who read widely and theorised, so as to strengthen his practice rather than being distracted from it. Nick, who died in 1996, had been an active trade unionist, a member of the Communist Party who turned to Trotsky. In 1968, he was expelled from the Australian Labour Party, because of his ecosocialist commitment, when he refused to support the building of a chemical waste facility in his working-class community:

> Origlass was elected to Leichhardt Council in the early '60s as an ALP member. He stood a good chance of winning preselection for the safe Labor seat of Balmain, but put principles before career. In 1968 he broke caucus discipline and opposed the installation of a dangerous chemical tank farm in Balmain. He was expelled from the ALP, together with his long-time comrade and fellow councillor Issy Wyner.
>
> They stood as Balmain Labor and were re-elected to the council, Origlass later being elected mayor of Leichhardt. He was re-elected mayor in 1972 following intensive red-baiting. A tied 6-6 vote on council resulted in him continuing as mayor after his name was drawn out of a hat. Origlass introduced the 'open council' principle for three years, giving residents the right to speak freely at council meetings and committees. (Percy (n.d.))

In later years, Nick was known during council meetings to turn off his hearing aid, when being rebuked by right-wing members of the council. It is impossible to identify a formula from Australia, that would turn activists into lifelong ecosocialist militants with a flair for effective strategy like Nick Origlass, or an antidote which might prevent the evolution of those like Peter Garrett who move into defence of the machine that is killing nature. However, ecosocialist action must engage with campaigns to defend local environments, recognising that environmental destruction is often aimed at working-class communities. Nick's work provides a small but encouraging example of effective ecosocialist action.

Ecosocialism must also engage with trade unions. Environmental problems are problems of production, and alternatives to destruction can be found first in the workplace. Indigenous struggles are vital and local communities must be defended against environmental damage globally, but workers are often dependent on industries that are polluting and destructive. Unless trade unionists are involved in ecosocialist politics, transformation will be impossible. Trade union work must be a real priority. To its credit, the Green Party of England and Wales has a strong trade union group, regularly provides solidarity with those taking industrial action and supports a trade union freedom bill. Trade unions in Britain were severely weakened by legislation from Mrs Thatcher's conservative government in the 1980s. Strong trade unions can carry out green struggles. Demands for alternative forms of production are very important: instead of weapons, why not produce wind turbines? Instead of cars, why not make buses or trains? In Britain, there is also a strong trade union climate-change group that brings together leading trade unionists, other climate activists, left groups and Green Party members. This is an area with which ecosocialists right around the world can be involved. When the wind-turbine manufacturer Vestas sought to close the only factory in Britain making wind-energy equipment, their workers occupied the plant and a wide variety of left and climate activists supported them. In Peru, the trade unions have defended the indigenous people, and Nick Origlass in his fight for his community was also rooted in trade union activism.

There are many potential contradictions. Many trade unionists have defended coal production, nuclear power and airport expansion. Greens have often ignored trade union struggles. Politics, especially ecosocialist politics, involves endless struggle.

In Britain, the former Rolls Royce worker Jerry Hicks ran for general secretary of one of the country's largest trade unions, Amicus-Unite, on a strongly ecosocialist programme, that opposed nuclear power and the expansion of Heathrow Airport and looked to create jobs via renewables, insulation and building new homes. Though he didn't win, he came a strong second, and his campaign was strongly supported by members of a variety of left groups and members of the Green Party.

Building support for similar trade union election campaigns is absolutely vital, and ecosocialists should be involved as much as they can with their unions. Ecosocialism demands workers' control of industry and the democratic planning of production. This is most advanced in Latin America, as a result of the economic crash of 2002, which has seen many firms in Argentina taken into workers' control. A good transitional ecosocialist demand would be to introduce legislation similar to that in Argentina, which allows workers to take control of failing businesses. In Venezuela, there has been a wave of factory occupations and the creation of thousands of cooperatives. Capitalism can be resisted and economic alternatives can be built now.

THE POVERTY OF THEORY

Ecosocialist action demands an element of ecosocialist theory. There is always in revolutionary politics a role for ideas, if action is to be appropriate and meaningful. Marx famously argued that if 'essences and appearances were identical', there would be no need for 'science'. What he meant was that if oppression was obvious and if the solutions to oppression were clear, there would be no need to look more deeply for theoretical explanations.

Without moving through a detailed discussion of the thoughts of Marx, Gramsci, Althusser, or Murray Bookchin and others, it is obvious that theoretical matters have very material consequences and must be attended to. The issue of agency is one example of why, despite criticism of abstract intellectual effort, theory is vitally important.

Green political theory has often been weak when it comes to the question of 'agency'. This question deals with the issue of which social group or groups are most likely to create change. Greens have often ignored strategic questions in general, with sometimes disastrous results. It is not enough to see change as a product of election victories without a much wider process of change. Greens have often seen social class as irrelevant. This is because many Greens, but not all, see the working class as unsympathetic to environmental concerns because their employment depends on polluting industries. It is also because Greens believe that all of us, in the end, will be harmed by catastrophic environmental change, and thus we all have a potential interest in green political change. 'Species' interest replaces specific class interest.

With the changes that have shifted much industrial production to China, India and other newly industrialised parts of the world, many Marxists or former Marxists, have become sceptical that the traditional working class can create fundamental social change. They have often put their hopes in 'new social movements', based on identity politics rather than material demands. This approach was taken by academics such as Laclau and Mouffe (1985). While perhaps superficially attractive, it gives rise to some serious problems.

One obvious problem with this rejection of working-class agency, is that far from being abolished or made irrelevant by globalisation and new forms of production, the working class still work to produce goods and services. Commodities which are bought don't magically appear out of thin air. We may live in an economy which is more dependent on knowledge and culture than in previous years, but goods still must be made and they are made by workers. Another problem is that it is wrong to see environmental issues as 'post-materialist'. Clean water, breathable air, a climate that functions to sustain comfortable human existence and that of other species are all 'material' issues. Environmental problems are not accidental, they are to a large extent products of a capitalist economic system that exploits both workers and the natural environment.

Social movements are vital but they are not necessarily 'new' nor can their concerns be neatly divided from supposed material questions. It is certainly inadequate to state that people in general will be motivated and able to bring about the social change necessary. It is clear that some social groups are more motivated to stop the locomotive and that different social groups have different levels of access to the engine room. Agency remains of great importance in discussing strategy.

As we have already suggested, indigenous people and workers are likely to be in a strong position to achieve change because they are most involved in the production and reproduction of the forces that shape the environment. Indigenous people, time after time, in the examples catalogued in this book, live in vital ecosystems and through systems of communal control have found ways of maintaining them, both to provide for their own needs and to preserve them. While there are examples of indigenous people damaging the environment, these are much rarer than examples of corporations *sustaining* the environment. Indigenous people are highly motivated to work for ecological survival. Often the environmental sentiments of indigenous people are noted, the point is that they have developed an environmental ethic, because of their material need to maintain the environment. In general, those who are dependent on a local level on the environment will have an interest in managing it ecologically.

AGENTS OF CHANGE

There is evidence to show that indigenous communities are acting as an increasingly self-confident and well-organised vanguard of ecosocialism right across our planet. Their concerns and efforts illustrate some very useful insights from Marx: that materialism and class are likely to remain of vital importance. Lived experience is vital to mobilisation; abstract appeals to new social movements are less important than struggles with an immediate effect on communities.

Workers, it is argued, benefit from polluting technology because it provides jobs, so will have little interest in environmental issues. However, pollution affects workers more directly than any other group in society, so workers have an interest in developing cleaner forms of production. As we have already noted, workers are likely to have technical knowledge and as they are involved in the production process, are potentially in a position to change it. Joel Kovel has, incidentally, argued that one of the most striking forms of enclosure is the enclosure of our labour power (2007: 247). Work must be made free and creative. The examples of Nick Origlass, Jerry Hicks and the green trade union movement of Australia, all provide examples of working-class green agency that leads to strong practical action for change.

In Britain, one of the most dynamic and sophisticated movements for ecological resistance has been the climate camp. Climate campers have physically resisted the construction of new coal-fired power stations, the expansion of airports and other large-scale projects that increase greenhouse gas emissions. In 2007, they camped close to Heathrow Airport, while in 2008, three thousand campers set up a week-long camp as a based to use direct action against the Kingsnorth coal-fired power station in Kent. In 2009, they camped twice in the financial centre of London. Climate campers take land, very much like the landless movements in Latin America, albeit temporarily, and they face repression. In the spring of 2009, police action against the camp, which had set up in London's financial centre, led to the death of passerby Ian Tomlinson.

The climate camp is instructive for a number of reasons. First, it is explicitly anti-capitalist and critical of carbon trading. It is able to mobilise thousands of people to take non-violent direct action. It organises in a grassroots democratic fashion and the camps provide an inspiring example of how to run events in a participatory way. It might be thought of as an example of broadly 'new social movement' activity. However, while it brings together many different kinds of people, it is explicitly focused on making links with working-class activists and indigenous people. In many ways, the climate camp in Britain, while rejecting labels and inspired more by anarchism than socialism, is a living example of ecosocialism in action. Ecosocialists are active in the climate camps in Britain, as well as in Belgium and Australia.

Of course, it is impossible to solve the debate on agency in a few paragraphs. But an obvious starting-point is to stress the vital importance of working-class and indigenous agency. Those most directly involved in production are likely to have the biggest potential to create ecological change and social change. It would clearly be a mistake to ignore others engaged in struggle by arguing that only certain social groups have the potential to create change, but it would be equally problematic to ignore the issue of agency. It is not enough to say people in general will create the change needed.

Another area where questions of theory are vital is the very notion of ecology as a science. While the majority of ecosocialists are unlikely to be active scientific researchers, ecological understanding is vital, if we are to transform society so as to maintain the natural environment. Ecosystems are complex chains of interrelationships: well-motivated actions can have unforeseen consequences. Environmental protection cannot be based purely on a wish to protect the environment. Engels' observation of the unintended consequences if we ignore ecology has been noted in an earlier chapter. A good example of where environmental concern which is not backed by more profound observation can be damaging is in regard to slash-and-burn cultivation. This method has been demonised and used as an excuse for enclosure, yet both scientific investigation and lengthy observation by the communities who undertake it suggests it is actually good practice and maintains forests.

Some environmentalists promote 'deep ecology' ideas, or perhaps a distortion of deep ecology that argues for the preservation of wilderness, areas of nature free from all human activity. Yet research shows that the whole of the Amazon to take one example has been shaped by human activity, that is, human beings are also part of nature (Montgomery 2007: 143).

Although much environmental destruction does not involve scientific understanding or even observation from non-scientists, 'theory' in the broadest senses is important. Ecosocialists should learn a little ecology or speak with those who know more.

Economics is another area where theory is vital. There are many myths about the market which are believed to be true. Increasingly, individuals are aware that capitalism is unsustainable, unjust and crisis ridden, but it is widely believed that capitalism is the only possible economic scenario. Ecosocialists need to educate themselves as to the alternatives based on the democratic commons. Equally, development and growth in capitalism can lead to poverty rather than prosperity. This is yet another area where much of Marx's work written in the nineteenth century is more sophisticated than much published more recently.

Theory in areas such as economics and ecology is also important: one failing of some attempts to construct a red-green politics is that left groups often move away from socialism, simply to adopt what they perceive as off-the-shelf forms of environmental or new social movement demands. Ecosocialist politics requires theoretical practice, because it demands re-evaluation of many assumptions, from the neutrality of technology to the benefits of economic growth. Interestingly, much of this re-evaluation can involve returning to the writings of Marx and Engels, which often contain forgotten insights. Marx's interest in indigenous people, in ecology and in the commons, for example, show that while he lived in the nineteenth century he was a twenty-first-century thinker.

Above all, theoretical work takes us back to the debate about change. Avoiding theory for the sake of theory, avoiding entry into the theoretical labyrinth as a way of compensating for lack of real political effect, avoiding theory as a form of boundary maintenance, ecosocialists need to ask and re-ask Lenin's question: 'What is to be done?' While answers are likely to vary from Lenin's and different conclusions will be made by different ecosocialists, the crisis we are in requires that this question is foremost.

LEARNING FROM LATIN AMERICA

The way that this question has been partially answered in Latin America, where traditional Marxist groups and green parties have not been central to the recent process of radical change, has been through the growth of powerful social movements. Movements based on radical democratic demands, with feminism, ecology and even new sexual identities, have been central. However such movements have been materialist and based on intense struggle in Latin America, which as we have seen stretch back for centuries. They have been materialist in that they stem from the demand of poor and particularly indigenous and other non-white citizens for a real share of wealth and democratic participation in countries dominated by elites. The notion that a single vanguard political party, equipped with the correct theory, is needed to lead such movements has not been apparent in Latin America. Social movement activity in its own right has been tremendously powerful. Economic and ecological crisis is likely to accelerate the creation of imaginative and diverse social movements on a global basis. Participating in dynamic social movement activity is yet another vital element of ecosocialist political practice.

However, the idea that social movement activity is sufficient is also inadequate. The political philosophy of autonomists such as John Holloway (2002), and Michael Hardt and Tony Negri (2001), looks highly attractive in comparison to the arid sectarianism of many far-left groups and to the compromises of political parties who seem often to move swiftly from radical rhetoric to a reality that maintains the machine. For Holloway, the scream is enough. For Negri and Hardt, the multitude will take power without the mediation of political organisation; in fact, for the authors of *Empire*, political parties and trade unions are policemen and women who discipline the productive energy of the people. From the perspective of Negri, Hardt and Holloway, formal political organisations act to prevent change.

Ecosocialist politics, like other forms of revolutionary socialism, seeks the withering-away of the capitalist state and the creation of a directly democratic society. However, to get to this ecosocialist society, the state must be transformed; it cannot simply be ignored. This distinction between ecosocialist politics and anarchist autonomism is well captured in the title of Greg Wilpert's book *Changing Venezuela by Taking Power* (2007).

Ecosocialism needs an electoral element. In different parts of the world this could take the form of participation within green parties, socialist alliances, or new green-left political organisations. Confusingly in Britain, it currently takes all three forms. Socialist Resistance aspires to create a broad-based socialist party and have been active in the

Respect Party. Green Left are active in the Green Party; in turn, the Alliance for Green Socialism participates in elections. In France, ecosocialists are active in the Green Party and the New Anti-Capitalist Party, in Australia in the Socialist Alliance and the Green Party. Such participation is important but will take different forms in different countries. For example, in Australia, votes can be transferred from one party to another, which means there is more likely to be space for both the Green Party and the Socialist Alliance. In some countries, green parties are much more to the left than others; equally, socialist political parties may be sympathetic or otherwise to green politics. Die Linke in Germany, for example, might provide a more attractive home for ecosocialists than the Green Party and contains an ecosocialist grouping. Electoral politics also provides a way of promoting ideas. The assumption that electoral success will lead to a smooth ascent to governmental power is naive; green and left parties are likely first to participate in coalitions with less radical political parties and, as we have noted, time and time again, compromise is richly rewarded and radicalism punished. Electoral politics can discipline and punish radicals, so they are bent into new shapes, so as to fit into prevailing patterns of power which support continued capitalist expansion.

The experience of the German Greens, is just one example of the difficulties, inherent, even from those aware of the dangers, of electoral politics. Processes of rotation and grassroots control of parliamentarians have been reversed in nearly all green parties. Similar processes distorted the social democratic parties of the First International, while communist parties under Stalin came to be controlled by the few who instructed the many. There are no easy answers to this dilemma. Obedience to ecosocialism may often mean being disobedient to formal political parties. It might be said without irony that ecosocialist politics is about making Greens greener as much as greening socialist politics.

State-level power is necessary, however difficult it is to achieve, in order to transform the structures – legal, social, economic and even physical – necessary for the transition to an ecosocialist society. Even participation from a marginal position can raise the debate, slow the rate of destruction and help promote positive change. In Venezuela and Bolivia, social movement protest has translated into electoral movements that have won power. Such power has helped create more space for the participation of workers, the indigenous and the broad majority of citizens who previously had no access to decision making.

The Latin American process of change is varied, imperfect and only partially ecosocialist. But it has introduced positive change, whereas in much of the globe, political and economic power has become more and more centralised and most citizens have less and less influence. Ecosocialist change on the rest of the planet must be about putting progressive socialist, ecological and decentralist parties into power. This is difficult, but necessary.

Ecosocialism cannot be created in just one part of the world. If it were, it would soon be crushed by hostile corporate forces and would be, even if left alone, too limited to create the international change needed to protect the planet. However, it is unlikely that ecosocialism will win simultaneous victories in many countries across the planet at the same time. Again, Latin America has shown that as a bloc of countries shift to the left, more space is available for greater change. For example, while Brazil's Lula has often been a disappointment for ecosocialists, the victory of a very imperfect left in Brazil made it far more difficult for George Bush to intervene against Hugo Chavez in Venezuela. When the US backed a coup against Chavez, international support for his government, especially from Cuba, helped return him swiftly to power. In turn, Chavez's success has provided economic support for Cuba. Venezuela has even provided aid to indigenous communities in the US, albeit in the form of cheap oil!

The construction of broad social movement mobilisations with ecosocialist demands, with a key role within them for workers and the indigenous, is surely applicable in many parts of the world. In Europe, though far from radically ecosocialist, green-left parties are winning some measure of power. Greenland is presently governed by an indigenous socialist party, Iceland after its recent economic collapse has seen the creation of a green left-socialist alliance government and Norway is governed by a coalition that includes a green-left party. Generally though, the European green left has been less radical in power than that of Latin America.

BUILD IT NOW!

Ecosocialism needs an institutional existence, although perhaps a modest one. Ecosocialist action is strengthened by the creation of ecosocialist organisation. In Britain, the existence of several explicitly ecosocialist networks has had a positive effect, for example, in promoting radical politics in the Green Party and promoting more explicit environmental concern amongst left political activists and trade unionists. The creation in Australia of the *Green Left Weekly*, one of the most important political newspapers in the country, has been very significant; both for encouraging the Socialist Alliance to take up serious ecosocialist politics and for influencing the Green Party. *Green Left Weekly* is published by the Democratic Socialist Perspective, who are active in the Socialist Alliance. However non-DSP ecosocialists are also active, in the Green Party, Labor Party and other groups.

John Rice, a Green Party member has formed a local ecosocialist network in Adelaide:

> It's not a political party, it's a network that aims to help people clarify their ideas and probably conclude that socialist solutions are feasible, and perhaps are the only ones that will extricate the world from its current state.
>
> At the moment we have people who are members of the Greens, the Labor Party, Friends of the Earth, the Socialist Alliance, and a range of religious organizations – the diversity is extraordinary. We held our first meeting in October, with 24 people, and the size has since doubled.
>
> It was important to set up an 'intersection set' of the various progressive layers, parties and movements in this city. If we can bring socialists – and those interested in socialist perspectives – together, to thrash out ideas, and then return to our respective sites of activism, hopefully this will have a political 'ripple effect'. (Richmond 2008)

The very modest Ecosocialist International Network has allowed activists in different parts of the globe to communicate and learn from each while providing practical solidarity. For example, the links between Latin American ecosocialists and activists in other parts of the world has been mutually beneficial.

In Britain, both Green Left and Socialist Resistance are active in respectively the Green and Respect parties; the Green Party has two Members of the European Parliament and in 2010, Caroline Lucas became the party's first Westminster

MP. Respect lost their one Member of Parliament George Galloway at the 2010 General Election, but has a number of councillors at the local government level. Both organisations are active in indigenous support, trade union work and the climate camp movement. All of these varied activities promote ecosocialism in ways which would be less likely to occur without formally constituted ecosocialist networks. If ecosocialists in Britain only worked with ecosocialists, little would be achieved. The British experience also suggests that it is important, that while groups may have different political origins, traditions and sometimes quite major organizational differences, positive cooperation can create political progress.

The institutional existence of ecosocialism must be both real and paradoxically rather modest. The crisis we face is so immediate and pressing that work must be carried out with very diverse political movements, networks and parties. Political purity equals sterility. Ecosocialists need to work with Greens who are not socialists and socialists who are not green. Equally in many parts of the world, ecosocialism is not a label used but the daily political practice of strong efforts for ecology, social justice and direct democracy. Ecosocialists need to participate in indigenous organizations, trade unions and broad social movements where appropriate. So putting effort into creating specifically ecosocialist networks or political parties at the expense of working with others is inappropriate. None the less, while part of much broader campaigns, it would be equally wrong not to organise ecosocialist bodies that participate in broader movements for change.

Ecosocialists need to set up ecosocialist networks. These are vital for creating practical political alternatives. However, ecosocialists should participate flexibly with other Greens and other socialists, where possible. Ecosocialist politics is about struggles over land rights, where environmental destruction is linked to social injustice and human rights abuse. Ecosocialism is also centrally about building green trade union activity. Ecosocialists should be involved in self-education, the promotion of ecosocialist ideas and the development of ecosocialist theory. While manifestations of ecosocialist politics are likely to be very varied, the broad pattern in Latin America where social movement struggles have led to political victories at a state level provides the greatest hope. Indeed Bolivian President Evo Morales led the opposition to a watered down agreement at the Copenhagen Climate Conference and called a counter conference in April 2010 at Cochabamba to ferment global climate resistance.

Political parties will risk being seduced by power, more radical opponents risk being seduced by the pursuit of ideological purity, and academics may avoid action. The only way to attempt to overcome these traps is to build strong grassroots movements and to remain sceptical – but not so sceptical as to avoid activism. The Chilean political theorist Marta Harnecker has written a series of very useful articles examining what we can learn from the Latin American experience. While it is impossible to summarise her extensive and important analysis, she notes that the construction of political organisations which aim to take state power is needed. Such state power should be used to create a communal alternative based on popular participation. State politics must be based, however, on social movement strength; if the state replaces the social movements, those elected to create change are much more likely to be absorbed and corrupted. She argues that diversity must be linked to unity:

> Among the left, there continues to be a difficulty to work together while respecting differences. In the past, the tendency of political

organizations, especially parties that self-declare themselves as parties of the working class, was always towards homogenising the social base within which they carried out political work. If this attitude was once justified due to the past identity and homogeneity of the working class, today it is anachronistic when confronted with a working class that is quite differentiated, and with the emergence of a diversity of new social actors. Today, we increasingly have to deal with a unity based on diversity, on respect for ethnic and cultural differences, for gender and for the sense of belonging of specific collectives. (Harnecker 2009)

Ecosocialism must be part of a broad political project which will take diverse and often contradictory forms, working with others. Ecosocialists must continued to argue for ecosocialist ideas within broader movements. In Britain in the 1880s, the Social Democratic Federation membership card was designed by the ecosocialist William Morris, with a beautiful oak-tree motif and the words 'Educate, Agitate, Organize'. These words remind us of the tasks for those of us who follow Morris's politics today. The final chapter of this book looks at how these three key tasks can be resourced.

7
Resources for Revolution

The challenges are daunting; the reality they reflect is frightening. How do people respond? It is possible to assume any number of attitudes. Here are some I've encountered:

Resignation. All is lost.
Divine providence. It's in God's hands
Denial. What problem?
Paralysis. It's too overwhelming.
Muddling through. It's going to be all right, somehow.
Deflection. It's not my problem.
Solutionist. Answers can and must be found.

Speth 2008: 42

He was 81, deaf, almost blind, overweight and none too nimble, and there he was stranded on top of the fence. The political legend had returned to his Queensland home town to head a protest against a proposed nuclear-waste dump and was leading the crowd over the high fence when he got stuck.

Greenland 1998: vii

There are many books on socialism, many books on green politics and even some that cover both ecology and socialism. This book is different in that it is an explicit call to non-violent arms. If having read this far, you are not involved with practical ecosocialist politics, whether taking part in peaceful direct action, helping on a strike picket line, spreading the word about indigenous struggles or supporting an election campaign, then my words will have failed me.

This chapter, like the entire book, intends to promote solid focused action. When you put this book down, you might want to log on to the Web and contact an organisation or, if not already doing so, get involved in active participation to build an ecologically sustainable and just world.

GROUPS, PARTIES, NETWORKS, MOVEMENTS

The most important resource is a network, group, political party, or other form of organisation. In Britain, where I am based, for example, Green Left <http://greenleftblog.blogspot.com/> is a network of ecosocialists active in the Green Party of England and Wales.

There are, of course, green parties in many parts of the world – some are more sympathetic to ecosocialist ideas, others less so. There is a central website of green parties <http://www.globalgreens.org/parties>. Green Left in Britain works with another ecosocialist organisation Socialist Resistance <http://socialistresistance.org/>, which is a part of the Fourth International. The Fourth International has also become supportive of the broad process of political change occurring in Latin America and is committed to supporting indigenous struggles. Details of different national sections of the FI can be found at <http://www.internationalviewpoint. org/spip.php?rubrique19>.

There are a number of red-green political parties outside the Green Party and the FI, including Norway's Socialist Left Party and the Icelandic Green Left Movement. In northern Europe, most of these red-green parties are members of the Nordic Green Left <http://www.guengl.eu>. The British-based Alliance for Green Socialism can be found at <http://www. greensocialist.org.uk/ags/>.

The Emerald Forum is the working title of a new left Green Party which is being built by former members of the Irish Green Party, disillusioned by its coalition with the right-wing Fianna Fail Party. The Emerald Forum's coordinator is Pat Kavanaugh, an Independent Green councillor from Wicklow, who can be contacted at <emeraldforum@gmail.com>.

The US Green Party can be contacted at <http://www. gp.org/index.php>. While there is no distinct ecosocialist party in the US, the International Socialist Organisation <http://www.internationalsocialist.org/>, Solidarity <http:// www.solidarity-us.org/> and Socialist Action <http://www. socialistaction.org/> work to promote ecosocialism. The US green radical magazine *Synthesis/Regeneration* is well worth reading on a regular basis and contains many articles from an ecosocialist perspective <http://www.greens.org/s-r/>. In the US, there is overlap between the Green Party and left groups. Also in the US, the Institute of Social Ecology which was founded by Murray Bookchin remains active <http:// www.social-ecology.org/>.

The Australian *Green Left Weekly* can be found at <http:// www.greenleft.org.au>. There are a number of ecosocialist networks in Germany. Ecosocialist Initiative <http://www. oekosozialismus.net/> is a small group which develops ecosocialist ideas; Ecological Left <http://www.oekologis-che-linke.de/> is an ecosocialist political party, and SALZ (Soziales-Arbeit-Leben-Zukunf) <http://www.schueren.1a-7936.antagus.de/> is an educational foundation that recently held an ecosocialist conference. There is also an ecosocialist group in the German Left Party <http://www.oekologische-plattform.de/>.

The Swiss ecosocialist party La Gauche can be found at <http://www.la-gauche.ch/>. You can discover more about ecosocialism in Greece via <http://ecosocialistsgreece.blogspot.com/> (in Greek) or <http://ecosocialists.webs.com/> (in English). The Romanian Ecosocialist Party can be contacted via their website <http://ecorom.webs.com/>. Turkish ecosocialists have websites at <www.yesilvesol.org> and <http://www.ekolojistler.org/ and a communication list <http://groups.yahoo.com/group/yesilvesol/>. In Italy, Ecorise is a useful ecosocialist website <http://ecorise.org/>.

In Canada, the 'New Socialist Group' which is committed to supporting 'ecological struggles and works to develop an ecological socialism from below', can be found at <http://www.newsocialist.org/>. Also in Canada, Socialist Voice produces some excellent ecosocialist and indigenous resources, functioning as a loose network rather than a centralist group <www.socialistvoice.com>. In Quebec, there is a distinct ecosocialist party Quebec Solidaire <www.quebecsolidaire.net.>

In Latin America, there are a number of twenty-first-century-style socialist parties, the most important being the Venezuelan United Socialist Party. But the most significant political organisations mobilising for ecosocialism are indigenous networks. In the Peruvian Amazon, the most important is Aidesep <www.aidesep.org.pe/>. *Lucha*

Indigena, published by Hugo Blanco, is a very good source of news about indigenous struggles <www.luchaindigena. com/> for those who read Spanish. Ecosocialists in Argentina produce a Marx and ecology blog at <www.marxismoecologico.blogspot.com>. The MST movement can be found at <http://www.mstbrazil.org/>.

In Britain, for those who are sceptical of political parties or want to supplement their activism with a commitment to non-violent direct action, a robust series of networks has evolved since the early 1990s, committed to direct action, anti-capitalism and ecology. The present form is the climate camp, a form which has extended to Australia, New Zealand, Ireland, the US and Ecuador <http://www.climatecamp.org. uk/>.

In other parts of the world, traditional left parties might be better able to carry the ecosocialist flag; take your pick, but get involved, or form an ecosocialist network.

EDUCATION

There are, of course, a vast array of education resources. I still feel, having read it way back in the early 1980s, the best single book on ecosocialism remains Alan Roberts' *The Self-Managing Environment* (1979). It covers many of the key themes, is short and readable as well as, like this book, being linked to practical struggles. The problems with capitalist growth, the battle for the commons, an ecosocialist perspective on science and an exploration of the green elements of Marx's thought are all included. Above all, it argues that the alternative to capitalism must be based on self-management through a radical scheme of political and economic democracy.

Joel Kovel's *The Enemy of Nature* (2007) is an up-to-date guide to ecosocialism which centres on climate change and shows us that the fiend without a face gnawing away at the future is the present economic system. Kovel edits the journal *Capitalism Nature Socialism* <www.cnsjournal.org/>. John Bellamy Foster's *Marx's Ecology* (2000) is a must read as well; it is a detailed examination of Marx's central concern with ecology. Foster's numerous books are very useful from an ecosocialist perspective; the most recent to deal with green politics is *The Ecological Revolution* (2009). He continues to edit *Monthly Review* which is another vital ecosocialist journal <www.monthlyreview.org/>.

Debal Deb's *Beyond Developmentality* (2009) examines ecology and the restoration of the commons. The concept of commons is covered perhaps best in The Corner House publication *Reclaiming the Commons*, which can also be found online <http://www.thecornerhouse.org.uk/item.shtml?x=52004>. Peter Linebaugh's work on the commons, *The Magna Carta Manifesto: Liberties and Commons for All* (2008), is also clear, inspiring and useful, and the careful empirical research undertaken by the Nobel Prize winner Professor Elinor Ostrom in her book *Governing the Commons* is vitally important. Open source and free software is everywhere, <http://www.benkler.org/> is a good start, along with <http://blog.p2pfoundation.net/>.

There are numerous excellent books on Marx and Engels. It continues to surprise me how in the nineteenth century, Marx and Engels grappled with problems and issues such as globalisation, the commons and ecology, which are essential issues in the twenty-first century. The Marxist Internet

Archive contains virtually all of Marx's and Engels' writings. The archive contains 40 different languages and as well as our bearded heroes, provides archives of 400 other left thinkers <www.marxists.org/>.

Andrew Dobson's *Green Political Thought* (2007) provides an excellent introduction to green politics, while a recently published guide to green economics is Tim Jackson's book *Prosperity without Growth* (2009).

Ecology remains a vast area and environmental concern is not enough – an understanding of the complexity of ecological issues is essential. A good start if one wishes to examine the global environmental crisis is James Speth's book *A Bridge at the End of the World* (2007). There are numerous good introductions to the science of ecology. Websites including Ecological Internet have information about key environmental campaign issues, http://www.ecologicalinter-net.org/campaigns/>.

Many ecosocialist publications are either in English or Spanish, but a useful introductory book on ecosocialism has recently been published in German by Klaus Engert, *Ökosozialismus – das geht* (Ecosocialism – it works).

CLIMATE JUSTICE

A useful ecosocialist resource is *The Global Fight for Climate Justice* (2009), a collection of 46 essays edited by Ian Angus on climate action, with contributions from writers as varied as Evo Morales, Fidel Castro, John Bellamy Foster, Joel Kovel and Hugo Blanco.

The Climate Justice site can be found here <http://www. climate-justice-action.org/>.

REPERTOIRES AND ACTIONS

How can we build practical movements that create vital change and how can we do so quickly? Social movement theory provides a number of important insights as to how movements can be created and grow. The intersection between what are the American and European schools of social movement can provide a powerful guide which can be used by movements to mobilise supporters, win battles and create social transformation. Sadly, it seems to be little known by movement activists. The American school evolved to examine how resources, including activists, repertoires of action and even culture, can be used to build effective networks. The European school stressed the structural elements of wider social and economic change in shaping movement development. The two fused to provide a useful synthesis dealing with how movements frame their messages, exploit pre-existing networks and make use of political opportunities. There is of course a huge literature, but it is worth using as a way of resourcing effective action.

My own book *Earth First! and the Anti-Roads Movement* (Wall 1999) looks at how radical environmentalists used non-violent direct action to successfully challenge a huge proposed expansion of motorways and major roads in Britain. Based on detailed research, the book shows how activists succeeded in building a powerful but flexible movement. Their success has fed into a wider anti-capitalist movement and the climate camps.

A classic of social movement theory is Sidney Tarrow's book *Power in Movement* (1998). In the 1980s, women peace activists created the Greenham Common Peace Camp to protest against first-strike nuclear cruise missiles. Sasha Roseneil, an academic researcher who as a teenager took part in the camp's activities has produced an excellent account of the movement in her book *Disarming Patriarchy* (1995). The anthropologist L. Shane Greene's book *Customizing Indigeneity* (2009) examines how the Peruvian Amazonian peoples built powerful political organisations and used them to defeat assaults on the rainforest and its peoples. Marta Harnecker's book *Rebuilding the Left* (2007) applies the experience of the Latin American left and social movements to the question of creating a left capable of introducing democratic and deep social change.

TRADE UNIONS

The Campaign against Climate Change (CaCC) trade union group set up a commission to examine how one million new jobs could be created in Britain by introducing renewable energy and other policies to move to a low-carbon future. The interim report 'One million climate jobs Now!' can be downloaded here <http://www.campaigncc.org/greenjobs >.

The Green Party of England and Wales have a dynamic trade union group with a blog and website <http://gptublog. blogspot.com/>. In the US, Labor for Sustainability seeks to link union activism and environmental issues <http://www. labor4sustainability.org/>.

WEBS AND BLOGS

Virtually all the organisations and networks mentioned here have websites; in addition, Ian Angus runs the excellent Climate and Capitalism site <http://climateandcapitalism.com/>.

Intercontinental Cry is one of many excellent indigenous websites <http://intercontinentalcry.org/>. The Ecosocialist International Site is <www.ecosocialistnetwork.org>. Real Climate covers the work of working climate scientists and is very useful for challenging the sceptics who tell us not to worry as the world heats up <www.realclimate.org/>.

FILMS

A number of excellent films offer more information about ecosocialism and might provide the basis for a good ecosocialist public event to draw in new activists. While I feel that listening to Roberto Perez is an even more exciting experience, *The Power of Community* is an excellent introduction to the green alternative constructed in Cuba during the 1990s, when cheap oil from the Soviet Union ceased to flow. John Bellamy Foster has alerted me to the film *Burn!*:

> Pontecorvo's epic film can be seen as a political and ecological allegory intended for our time. It is set in the early nineteenth century on an imaginary Caribbean island called *Burn*. *Burn* is a Portuguese slave colony with a sugar production monoculture dependent on the export of sugar as a cash crop to the world economy. In the opening scene we are informed that the island got its name from the fact that the only way that the original Portuguese colonizers were able to vanquish the indigenous population was by setting fire to the entire island and killing everyone on it, after which slaves were imported from Africa to cut the newly planted sugar cane. (Burn 2007)

The 1980s television series *A Very British Coup* and the more recent (2003) Irish film examining the coup against Chavez, *Chavez: Inside the Coup* (in the US, *The Revolution will not be televised*) are good accounts of how powerful elites might react to ecosocialist attempts to create change. Pablo Navarette's film *Inside the Revolution* looks at the process of building communal power in Venezuela. *Milk*, Gus Van Sant's film about the late, great gay politician Harvey Milk is also a great introduction to practical organisation and the repression faced by those who want to change the world.

Owen Clayton, a member of Green Left, made the following suggestions:

> *Winstanley* – 1975 – about the Diggers movement during the English Civil War.
>
> *The Grapes of Wrath* – obvious choice I guess, but relevant given dust bowl. Or you could recommend the book.
>
> *Matewan* – classic depiction of US miners' struggle.
>
> *Rosa Blanca* – released 1961 but banned until 1972 – synopsis: 'an illiterate Indian (Ignacio Lopez Tarso) lives an idyllic existence as a landowner on Mexico's Gulf Coast until the greed of a US oil company gets in the way'.
>
> *The Wizard of Oz* – given its original allegorical status, *The Wizard of Oz* was originally an allegory about the power of money and the hollowness of the tiny frame behind the throne issuing orders. (personal correspondence)

Pete Murray, also from Green Left, suggested *Derzu Uzala* 'which is an interesting film about a Siberian indigenous hunter made by the great Japanese director Akira Kurosawa' (personal correspondence). Kurosawa's series of short films *Dreams* also contains some powerful anti-nuclear and green statements. I am sure readers can think of more films relevant to ecosocialism and in a multi-media open source world we can make our own. Not being a film-maker, I am unable to recommend practical guides to film-making but I am sure others will take up the challenge. Resources should not be limited to texts and websites. Well, I could continue on to permaculture, green building, how to print and publish leaflets, green novels and ecocriticism but hopefully this sketch will encourage readers to get active, organise and spread ideas.

Engels suggested that 'An ounce of action is worth a ton of theory'; in such a spirit, I hope you can use the words here to help fuel some practical activity. We have a world to save. Non-action is the road to extinction; contemplation is a luxury in a world where temperatures are rising.

Appendix 1
The Belém Ecosocialist Declaration

This document is a second draft of the Ecosocialist Manifesto, debated and endorsed at a meeting of the Ecosocialist International Network at the World Social Forum in Belém, Brazil between January 27ᵗʰ and February 1ˢᵗ, 2009

> 'The world is suffering from a fever due to climate change, and the disease is the capitalist development model.' – Evo Morales, president of Bolivia, September 2007

HUMANITY'S CHOICE

Humanity today faces a stark choice: ecosocialism or barbarism.

We need no more proof of the barbarity of capitalism, the parasitical system that exploits humanity and nature alike. Its sole motor is the imperative toward profit and thus the need for constant growth. It wastefully creates unnecessary products, squandering the environment's limited resources and returning to it only toxins and pollutants. Under capitalism, the only measure of success is how much more is sold every day, every week, every year – involving the creation of vast quantities of products that are directly harmful to both humans and nature, commodities that cannot be produced without spreading disease, destroying the forests that produce the oxygen we breathe, demolishing ecosystems, and treating our water, air and soil like sewers for the disposal of industrial waste.

Capitalism's need for growth exists on every level, from the individual enterprise to the system as a whole. The insatiable hunger of corporations is facilitated by imperialist expansion in search of ever greater access to natural resources, cheap labor and new markets. Capitalism has always been ecologically destructive, but in our lifetimes these assaults on the earth have accelerated. Quantitative change is giving way to qualitative transformation, bringing the world to a tipping point, to the edge of disaster. A growing body of scientific research has identified many ways in which small temperature increases could trigger irreversible, runaway effects – such as rapid melting of the Greenland ice sheet or the release of methane buried in permafrost and beneath the ocean – that would make catastrophic climate change inevitable.

Left unchecked, global warming will have devastating effects on human, animal and plant life. Crop yields will drop drastically, leading to famine on a broad scale. Hundreds of millions of people will be displaced by droughts in some areas and by rising ocean levels in others. Chaotic, unpredictable weather will become the norm. Air, water and soil will be poisoned. Epidemics of malaria, cholera and even deadlier diseases will hit the poorest and most vulnerable members of every society.

The impact of the ecological crisis is felt most severely by those whose lives have already been ravaged by imperialism in Asia, Africa, and Latin America, and indigenous peoples everywhere are especially vulnerable. Environmental destruction and climate change constitute an act of aggression by the rich against the poor.

Ecological devastation, resulting from the insatiable need to increase profits, is not an accidental feature of capitalism: it is built into the system's DNA and cannot be reformed away. Profit-oriented production only considers a short-term horizon in its investment decisions, and cannot take into account the long-term health and stability of the environment. Infinite economic expansion is incompatible with finite and fragile ecosystems, but the capitalist economic system cannot tolerate limits on growth; its constant need to expand will subvert any limits that might be imposed in the name of 'sustainable development.' Thus the inherently unstable capitalist system cannot regulate its own activity, much less overcome the crises caused by its chaotic and parasitical growth, because to do so would require setting limits upon accumulation – an unacceptable option for a system predicated upon the rule: Grow or Die!

If capitalism remains the dominant social order, the best we can expect is unbearable climate conditions, an intensification of social crises and the spread of the most barbaric forms of class rule, as the imperialist powers fight among themselves and with the global south for continued control of the world's diminishing resources.

At worst, human life may not survive.

CAPITALIST STRATEGIES FOR CHANGE

There is no lack of proposed strategies for contending with ecological ruin, including the crisis of global warming looming as a result of the reckless increase of atmospheric carbon dioxide. The great majority of these strategies share one common feature: they are devised by and on behalf of the dominant global system, capitalism.

It is no surprise that the dominant global system which is responsible for the ecological crisis also sets the terms of the debate about this crisis, for capital commands the means of production of knowledge, as much as that of atmospheric carbon dioxide. Accordingly, its politicians, bureaucrats, economists and professors send forth an endless stream of proposals, all variations on the theme that the world's ecological damage can be repaired without disruption of market mechanisms and of the system of accumulation that commands the world economy.

But a person cannot serve two masters – the integrity of the earth and the profitability of capitalism. One must be abandoned, and history leaves little question about the allegiances of the vast majority of policy-makers. There is every reason, therefore, to radically doubt the capacity of established measures to check the slide to ecological catastrophe.

And indeed, beyond a cosmetic veneer, the reforms over the past thirty-five years have been a monstrous failure. Isolated improvements do of course occur, but they are inevitably overwhelmed and swept away by the ruthless expansion of the system and the chaotic character of its production.

One example demonstrates the failure: in the first four years of the 21st Century, global carbon emissions were nearly three times as great per annum as those of the decade of the 1990s, despite the appearance of the Kyoto Protocols in 1997.

Kyoto employs two devices: the 'Cap and Trade' system of trading pollution credits to achieve certain reductions in emissions, and projects in the global south – the so-called 'Clean Development Mechanisms' – to offset emissions in the highly industrialized nations. These instruments all rely upon market mechanisms, which means, first of all, that atmospheric carbon dioxide becomes a commodity under the control of the same interests that created global warming. Polluters are not compelled to reduce their carbon emissions, but allowed to use their power over money to control the carbon market for their own ends, which include the devastating exploration for yet more carbon-based fuels. Nor is there a limit to the amount of emission credits which can be issued by compliant governments.

Since verification and evaluation of results are impossible, the Kyoto regime is not only incapable of controlling emissions, it also provides ample opportunities for evasion and fraud of all kinds. As even the *Wall Street Journal* put it in March, 2007, emissions trading 'would make money for some very large corporations, but don't believe for a minute that this charade would do much about global warming.'

The Bali climate meetings in 2007 opened the way for even greater abuses in the period ahead. Bali avoided any mention of the goals for drastic carbon reduction put forth by the best climate science (90% by 2050); it abandoned the peoples of the global south to the mercy of capital by giving jurisdiction over the process to the World Bank; and made offsetting of carbon pollution even easier.

In order to affirm and sustain our human future, a revolutionary transformation is needed, where all particular struggles take part in a greater struggle against capital itself. This larger struggle cannot remain merely negative and anti-capitalist. It must announce and build a different kind of society, and this is ecosocialism.

THE ECOSOCIALIST ALTERNATIVE

The ecosocialist movement aims to stop and to reverse the disastrous process of global warming in particular and of capitalist ecocide in general, and to construct a radical and practical alternative to the capitalist system. Ecosocialism is grounded in a transformed economy founded on the non-monetary values of social justice and ecological balance. It criticizes both capitalist 'market ecology' and productivist socialism, which ignored the earth's equilibrium and limits. It redefines the path and goal of socialism within an ecological and democratic framework.

Ecosocialism involves a revolutionary social transformation, which will imply the limitation of growth and the transformation of needs by a profound shift away from quantitative and toward qualitative economic criteria, an emphasis on use-value instead of exchange-value.

These aims require both democratic decision-making in the economic sphere, enabling society to collectively define its goals of investment and production, and the collectivization of the means of production. Only collective decision-making and ownership of production can offer the longer-term perspective that is necessary for the balance and sustainability of our social and natural systems.

The rejection of productivism and the shift away from quantitative and toward qualitative economic criteria involve rethinking the nature and goals of production and economic activity in general. Essential creative, non-productive and reproductive human activities, such as householding, child-rearing, care, child and adult education, and the arts, will be key values in an ecosocialist economy.

Clean air and water and fertile soil, as well as universal access to chemical-free food and renewable, non-polluting energy sources, are basic human and natural rights defended by ecosocialism. Far from being 'despotic,' collective policy-making on the local, regional, national and international levels amounts to society's exercise of communal freedom and responsibility. This freedom of decision constitutes a liberation from the alienating economic 'laws' of the growth-oriented capitalist system.

To avoid global warming and other dangers threatening human and ecological survival, entire sectors of industry and agriculture must be suppressed, reduced, or restructured and others must be developed, while providing full employment for all. Such a radical transformation is impossible without collective control of the means of production and democratic planning of production and exchange. Democratic decisions on investment and technological development must replace control by capitalist enterprises, investors and banks, in order to serve the long-term horizon of society's and nature's common good.

The most oppressed elements of human society, the poor and indigenous peoples, must take full part in the ecosocialist revolution, in order to revitalize ecologically sustainable traditions and give voice to those whom the capitalist system cannot hear. Because the peoples of the global south and the poor in general are the first victims of capitalist destruction, their struggles and demands will help define the contours of the ecologically and economically sustainable society in creation. Similarly, gender equality is integral to ecosocialism, and women's movements have been among the most active and vocal opponents of capitalist oppression. Other potential agents of ecosocialist revolutionary change exist in all societies.

Such a process cannot begin without a revolutionary transformation of social and political structures based on the active support, by the majority of the population, of an ecosocialist program. The struggle of labour – workers, farmers, the landless and the unemployed – for social justice is inseparable from the struggle for environmental justice. Capitalism, socially and ecologically exploitative and polluting, is the enemy of nature and of labour alike.

Ecosocialism proposes radical transformations in:

- the energy system, by replacing carbon-based fuels and biofuels with clean sources of power under community control: wind, geothermal, wave, and above all, solar power.
- the transportation system, by drastically reducing the use of private trucks and cars, replacing them with free and efficient public transportation;
- present patterns of production, consumption, and building, which are based on waste, inbuilt obsolescence, competition and pollution, by producing only sustainable and recyclable goods and developing green architecture;
- food production and distribution, by defending local food sovereignty as far as this is possible, eliminating polluting industrial agribusinesses, creating sustainable agro-ecosystems and working actively to renew soil fertility.

To theorize and to work toward realizing the goal of green socialism does not mean that we should not also fight for concrete and urgent reforms right now. Without any illusions about 'clean capitalism,' we must work to impose on the powers that be – governments, corporations, international institutions – some elementary but essential immediate changes:

- drastic and enforceable reduction in the emission of greenhouse gases,
- development of clean energy sources,
- provision of an extensive free public transportation system,
- progressive replacement of trucks by trains,
- creation of pollution clean-up programs,
- elimination of nuclear energy, and war spending.

These and similar demands are at the heart of the agenda of the Global Justice movement and the World Social Forums, which have promoted, since Seattle in 1999, the convergence of social and environmental movements in a common struggle against the capitalist system.

Environmental devastation will not be stopped in conference rooms and treaty negotiations: only mass action can make a difference. Urban and rural workers, peoples of the global south and indigenous peoples everywhere are at the forefront of this struggle against environmental and social injustice, fighting exploitative and polluting multinationals, poisonous and disenfranchising agribusinesses, invasive genetically modified seeds, biofuels that only aggravate the current food crisis. We must further these social-environmental movements and build solidarity between anticapitalist ecological mobilizations in the North and the South.

This Ecosocialist Declaration is a call to action. The entrenched ruling classes are powerful, yet the capitalist system reveals itself every day more financially and ideologically bankrupt, unable to overcome the economic, ecological, social, food and other crises it engenders. And the forces of radical opposition are alive and vital. On all levels, local, regional and international, we are fighting to create an alternative system based in social and ecological justice.

Appendix 2
The Headcorn Declaration
from Green Left

Green Left is the ecosocialist network in the Green Party of England and Wales; this declaration is its founding statement from 2006.

Green Left has been launched as a network for socialists and other radicals in the Green Party of England and Wales. It will act as an outreach body that will communicate the party's radical policies to socialists and other anti-capitalists outside the party.

Green Left (GL) is based on the assumption that capitalism is a system that wrecks the planet and promotes war. A green society must be based on economic, political and social justice. GL in short works to promote ecosocialism as a solution to our planetary ills.

GL supports the democratic structures in the party and encourages transparency, accountability and engagement in all organs of the party. We also see the Green Party as a 'bottom up' political organisation where the principles of the membership are paramount and not a 'top down' one where a self-designated political elite decide on policies and principles.

GL aims to increase and improve the international links of the Green Party, building links with radical greens and ecosocialists across the planet. It will work closely with members of other European Green Parties to reform the workings of the European Green Party structures that must be democratised. Green politics must realise the slogan 'think globally, act locally' by linking practical local campaigns to global issues of ecology, democracy, justice and liberation.

GL aims to act within the Green Party so as to raise Green Party politics to meet the demands of its radical policies. Green politics needs to be based on dynamic campaigning and hard intellectual groundwork to create workable alternatives.

GL aims to build regional campaigns and contribute to coalition-building through coherent alignments and open discussion with progressive anti-capitalists. The movement that is required to address the issues across Britain, Europe and the world will not be the sole preserve of one party. The movement requires the development of united action by progressive forces including organisations formed by working people to defend their interests in the workplace. Within this diverse movement GL will stand firmly in favour of the libertarian and democratic traditions of ecosocialism.

It is vitally important that the Green Party works to develop the continuing peace, environmental and social movements. An orientation to organised working people through the Green Party Trade Union Group (GPTU) also requires maximum support from GL, with the emphasis on supporting radical and rank and file currents in the unions. Likewise, GL should seek to promote organisation and solidarity amongst currently unorganised and marginalised groups.

GL will work to enhance Green Party contributions to demonstrations, marches and other solidarity events. Greens must be active on issues that affect ordinary working people in their everyday lives and aim to be known as amongst their strongest defenders.

While GL is keen to build links with members of faith communities, and to fight alongside them against intolerance and discrimination, it will not compromise on human rights – including issues concerning women, the lesbian, gay, bisexual and transgender communities, and people with disabilities.

Since the activism of William Morris in the Social Democratic Federation and Socialist League in the late nineteenth century, there has been an ecosocialist tradition in Britain. Green Left believes that ecosocialism provides an alternative to a society based on alienation, economic exploitation, corporate rule, ecological destruction and wars. Our analysis demands that in the best tradition of the historic left we 'agitate, educate and organise' to build such an alternative.

The time has come for drawing together forces that can present a serious challenge to the disastrous neo-liberal project. We believe that 'another world is possible', based on ecological and socialist values. In conclusion, Green Left would work to enable you to live in a society based on peace, ecological balance, economic equality and inclusion. Come and join us!

Bibliography

ABC News (2009), 'Greens savage Garrett over uranium mine', *ABC News*, 15 July <http://www.abc.net.au/news/stories/2009/07/15/2625957.htm>.

Adorno, T. and Horkheimer, M. (1979), *The Dialectic of Enlightenment*. London: Verso.

Allen-Mills, T. (2007), 'Biofuels gangs kill for green profits', *Sunday Times Online*, 3 June <http://www.timesonline.co.uk/tol/news/world/us_and_americas/article1875709.ece)>.

Angus, I. (2009), *The Global Fight for Climate Justice*. London: Resistance Books.

Athanasiu, A. (2005), 'Greens divided over dissing feds', *Now Toronto*, 1 December, Vol. 25, No. 14 <http://www.nowtoronto.com/print.cfm?content=150802>.

Bahro, R. (1981), *The Alternative in Eastern Europe*. London: Verso.
—— (1984), *From Red to Green*. London: Verso.

Barteri, F. (2010), 'Ecorise Italy', *ecosocialism canada*, 4 March <http://ecosocialismcanada.blogspot.com/2010/03/ecorise-italy.html>.

Benjamin, J. (2009), 'Fund of hedge funds aims to profit from green movement', *Investment News*, 31 July <http://www.investmentnews.com/apps/pbcs.dll/article?AID=/20090731/REG/907319976/1020/STREETWISE>.

Benjamin, W. (1985), *One-Way Street and Other Writings*. London: Verso.

Benkler Y. (2006), *The Wealth of Networks*. London and New Haven, CT: Yale University Press.

Benton, T. (1993), *Natural Relations: Ecology, Animal Rights and Social Justice*. London: Verso.

Blake, W. (1977), *The Complete Poems*. London: Penguin.

Bond, P. and Dada, R. (2007), 'Who killed Sajida Khan?', *Green Left Weekly*, 20 July <http://www.greenleft.org.au/node/37984>.

Bookchin, M. (1974), *Toward an Ecological Society*. Montreal: Black Rose Books.

—— (1971), *Post-scarcity Anarchism*. San Francisco, CA: Ramparts Press.

Brodine, V.W. (1992), 'Green Cuba', *Multinational Monitor*, November <http://multinationalmonitor.org/hyper/issues/1992/11/mm1192_10.html>.

Bukharin, N. (2005), *Philosophical Arabesques*. New York: Monthly Review Press.

Burkett, P. (1999), *Marx and Nature*. New York: St Martins Press.

Campbell, MacGregor (2009), 'Meadows of the sea in "shocking" decline, *New Scientist*, 3 July <http://www.newscientist.com/article/dn17412-meadows-of-the-sea-in-shocking-decline.html>.

Carrell, S. (2002), 'Banks' £35m gift for WWF angers Greens', *Independent*, 7 April <http://www.independent.co.uk/environment/banks-acircpound35m-gift-for-wwf-angers-greens-656659.html>.

Castañeda, J. (1993), *Utopia Unarmed*. New York: Knopf.

Chestney, N. and Szabo, M. (2009), 'Global carbon market doubled in 2008, cut less CO_2', *Reuters*, 27 May <http://www.reuters.com/article/idUSTRE54Q17A20090527?feedType=RSS&feedName=environmentNews>.

Climate Camp 09 (2009), 'What is Carbon Trading?', 21 March <http://old.climatecamp.org.uk/?q=g20-why>.

Cohn-Bendit, D. and G. Cohn-Bendit (2000), *Obsolete Communism: The Left Wing Alternative*, Edinburgh, London and San Francisco, CA: AK Press.

Commoner. B. (1971), *The Closing Circle: Nature, Man, and Technology*. New York: Knopf.

Crace, J. (2009), 'The theory of everything', *Guardian*, 12 March <http://www.guardian.co.uk/society/2009/mar/12/equality-british-society>.

Cumming, E. (2010) 'The Biggest Dump in the World', *Daily Telegraph*, 16 March <http://www.telegraph.co.uk/science/7450769/The-Biggest-Dump-in-the-World.html>.

Davis, M. (2006), *The Monster at Our Door*. New York: Owl Books.

Deb, D. (2009), *Beyond Developmentality*. London: Earthscan.

Democratic Socialist Perspective (2009), 'Party-building perspectives report', *Democratic Socialist Perspective*, June <http://www.dsp.org.au/node/228>.

Dobson, A. (2007), *Green Political Thought*. London: Routledge.

The Ecologist (1992), *Whose Common Future? Reclaiming the Commons*. London: Earthscan.

The Economist (2009), 'An end to inequality?', 2 April <http://www.economist.com/research/articlesBySubject/displaystory.cfm?subjectid=423172&story_id=E1_TPPVGGVD>.

Edward Carpenter Archive (n.d.), 'Biographical Note', *Edward Carpenter Archive* <http://www.edwardcarpenter.net/ecbiog.htm>.

Engels, F. (1987), 'The Transition from Ape to Man', in Karl Marx and Frederick Engels, *Collected Works*. London: Lawrence and Wishart.

Engert, K. (2010), *Ökosozialismus – das geht [Ecosocialism – it works]*. Köln/Karlsruhe: Neuer isp-Verlag.

Enzensberger, H.M. (1974), 'A Critique of Political Ecology', *New Left Review*, I/84, March–April, pp. 3–31.

FAO (2006), 'Livestock impacts on the environment', Food and Agriculture Organization of the United Nations online magazine <http://www.fao.org/ag/magazine/0612sp1.htm>.

Forster, E.M. (1951), *Two Cheers for Democracy*. London: Edward Arnold.

Foster, J.B. (2000), *Marx's Ecology*. New York: Monthly Review Press.

—— (2007), 'The Ecology of Destruction', *Monthly Review*, Vol. 58, No. 8, February <http://www.monthlyreview.org/0207jbf.htm>.

—— (2009), *The Ecological Revolution*. New York: Monthly Review Press.

Fromm, E. (1961), *Marx's Concept of Man*. New York: Frederick Ungar Publishing.

—— (1979), *To Have or to Be*. London: Abacus.

Fuentes, F. (2009), 'Eco-socialist declaration, call for global network', *Green Left*, 23 January <http://www.greenleft.org.au/node/40923>.

Golinger, E. (2007), 'Venezuela's Green Agenda: Chavez should be named the "Environmental President"', *venezuelanalysis.com*, 27 February <http://venezuelanalysis.com/analysis/2244>.

Gorz, A. (1980), *Ecology as Politics*. Boston, MA: South End Press.

—— (1982), *Farewell to the Working Class*. London: Pluto Press.

Goudie, A. (1981) *The Human Impact on the Natural Environment.* Oxford: Blackwell.

Gould, P. (1988), *Early Green Politics.* Brighton: Harvester Press.

Greene, L.S. (2009), *Customizing Indigeneity.* Standford, CA: Stanford University Press.

Greenland, H. (1998), *Red Hot: The Life and Times of Nick Origlass.* Neutral Bay, Australia: Wellingon Lane Press.

Hardt, M. and Negri, A. (2001), *Empire.* New York: Harvard University Press.

Harnecker, M. (2007), *Rebuilding the Left.* London: Zed Press.

—— (2009), 'Ideas for the struggle #1 – Insurrections or revolutions? The role of the political instrument', *LINKS*, 21 May <http://links.org.au/node/1059>.

Harvey, F. and Fidler, S. (2007), 'Industry caught in carbon "smokescreen"', *Financial Times*, 25 April <http://www.ft.com/cms/s/0/48e334ce-f355-11db-9845-000b5df10621.html?nclick_check=1>.

Haywood, J. (2007), 'The Revolutionary Legacy of Thomas Sankara', *Socialist Resistance*, 48.

Herber, Lewis (1962), *Our Synthetic Environment.* New York: Knopf.

Hildyard, N. et al. (1995), 'Reclaiming the Commons', originally published in *The Ecologist*, available at <http://www.thecornerhouse.org.uk/item.shtml?x=52004#conclusion>.

Hockenos, P. (2008), *Joschka Fischer and the making of the Berlin Republic.* Oxford: Oxford University Press.

Holender, A. (2006), *Zentrepreneurism.* Vancouver: Write Action Publishing.

Holloway, J. (2002), *Change the World Without Taking Power.* London: Pluto Press.

Hopkins, R. (2008), *The Transition Handbook.* Dartington: Green Books.

Hughes, J. (2000), *Ecology and Historical Materialism.* Cambridge: Cambridge University Press.

Hülsberg, W. (1988), *The German Greens.* London: Verso.

Hürriyet Daily News and Economic Review (2010), 'Turkish advertising sector on the way to recovery', 31 March <http://www.

hurriyetdailynews.com/n.php?n=advertising-sector-on-the-way-to-recovery-2010-03-31>.

Independent (2009), '1,500 farmers commit mass suicide in India', *Independent*, 15 April 2009 <http://www.independent.co.uk/news/world/asia/1500-farmers-commit-mass-suicide-in-india-1669018.html>.

Innovation (2007),'Indigenous people lash out at climate talks', *Innovation* website, 7 December <http://www.iol.co.za/index.php?sf=116&set_id=1&click_id=31&art_id=nw20071207195516785C556709>.

Jackson, T. (2009), *Prosperity without Growth*. London: Earthscan.

Jensen, D. (2009), 'Forget Shorter Showers', *Orion*, July/August <http://www.orionmagazine.org/index.php/articles/article/4801/%29>.

Kellner, D. (1982), 'Marcuse, Liberation, and Radical Ecology', *Illuminations*, 5 April <http://www.uta.edu/huma/illuminations/kell11.htm>.

Klein, N. (2009), 'What might the world look like if the bail out works? Like Sarah Palin', *Guardian*, 30 July <http://www.guardian.co.uk/commentisfree/2009/jul/30/sarah-palin-capitalism-climate>.

Klimaat Actie Kamp (2009), 'Wie zijn we?' <http://www.klimaatactiekamp.org/index.php?option=com_content&view=article&id=46&Itemid=57>.

Kneen, B. (2002), *Invisible Giant: Cargill and Its Transnational Strategies*. London: Pluto Press.

Komarov, B. (1980), *The Destruction of Nature in the Soviet Union*. London: Pluto Press.

Kovel, J. (1998), 'Negating Bookchin', in *Social Ecology after Bookchin*. New York: Guildford Press.

—— (2007), *The Enemy of Nature*. London: Zed Press.

—— and Löwy, M. (2001), *The Ecosocialist Manifesto* <http://www.ecosocialistnetwork.org/Docs/EcoManifesto.htm>.

Krader, L. (1972), *The Ethnological Notebooks of Karl Marx*. Assen, NE: Van Gorcum.

Laclau, E. and Mouffe, C. (1985), *Hegemony and Socialist Strategy*. London: Verso.

La Soja Mata (2006), 'Silvina Talavera Campaign: Vistory at high price', *La Soja Mata*, 20 November <http://lasojamata.iskra.net/en/node/18>.

Leber, J. (2009), 'Riding a Wave of Culture Change, DOD Strives to Trim Energy Demand', *New York Times*, 20 July <http://www. nytimes.com/cwire/2009/07/20/20climatewire-riding-a-wave-of-culture-change-dod-strives-23689.html>.

Linebaugh P. (2008), *The Magna Carta Manifesto: Liberties and Commons for All*. Berkeley: University of California Press.

Lipietz, A. (1995), *Green Hopes*. Cambridge: Polity Press.

Lohmann, L. (2009), 'Uncertainty Markets and Carbon Markets', *The Corner House* <http://www.thecornerhouse.org.uk/summary. shtml?x=565040>.

Löwy, M. (2009), 'Ecosocialism', *ZNet*, 19 July <http://www. zcommunications.org/ecosocialism-by-michael-lowy>.

Ma'anit, A. (2006), 'If you go down to the woods today ... ', *New Internationalist*, July, No. 391.

Marcuse, H. (1966), *Eros and Civilisation*. Boston, MA: Beacon Press.
—— (1991), *One Dimensional Man*. London: Routledge.

Marsden, R. (2009), 'Lucas Aerospace – When workers planned production', *Socialist Resistance*, August <http://links.org.au/ node/1216>.

Marx, K. (1981), *Capital*. Vol. 3. New York: Vintage.
—— and Engels, F. (1975), *Karl Marx, Frederick Engels: Collected Works*. London: Lawrence and Wishart.

McIlroy, J. (2009), 'Hugo Chavez speaks to GLW bureau: Socialism will save world', *Green Left Weekly*, 16 May <http://www.greenleft. org.au/node/41652>.

Mitchell, T. (2009), 'China Bows to Activist Pressure on Plant', *Financial Times*, 31 July <http://www.ft.com/cms/s/0/ef00fc42-7d69-11de-b8ee-00144feabdc0.html?nclick_check=1>.

Montgomery, D. (2007), *Dirt: The Erosion of Civilizations*. Berkeley and Los Angeles: University of California Press.

Morales, E. (2009), 'Respect Mother Earth!', in Angus, I., *The Global Fight for Climate Justice*. London: Resistance Books.

Morris, B. (1990), 'The Death of the Aral Sea', *Multinational Monitor*, 'USSR in Crisis' issue, Vol. 11, No. 9 < http://multinationalmonitor. org/hyper/issues/1990/09/morris.html>.

Morris, W. (2004), *Art and Socialism*. London: Kessinger.

Newman, R. (2006), 'It's capitalism or a habitable planet – you can't have both', *Guardian*, 2 February <http://www.guardian.co.uk/environment/2006/feb/02/energy.comment>.

Ngũgĩ wa Thiong'o (2006), *The Wizard of the Crow*. London: Harvill Secker.

Ostrom, E. (1990), *Governing the Commons*. Cambridge: Cambridge University Press.

—— (2006), '12 Questions to ... Elinor Ostrom', *Gaia Magazine*, April, pp. 246–7 <http://www.indiana.edu/~workshop/reprints/gaia.pdf>.

—— (2008), 'Crafting Rules to Sustain Resources', *Academy Blog* <http://blog.aapss.org/index.cfm?commentID=58>.

Pan, Y. (2007), 'Pan Yue on Ecosocialism and China's Environmental Crisis', *Climate and Capitalism*, 20 April <http://climateandcapitalism.com/?p=74>.

Pannekoek, A. (1933), 'Destruction as a Means of Struggle' <http://marxists.org/archive/pannekoe/1933/destruct.htm>.

Paul, R. (2007), 'Venezuelan government to sell Linux-based computers', *ars technica* website, 18 June <http://arstechnica.com/old/content/2007/06/venezuelan-government-to-sell-linux-based-computers.ars>.

Pearce, F. (2006), 'No more seafood by 2050?', *New Scientist*, 02 November 2006 <http://www.newscientist.com/article/dn10433-no-more-seafood-by-2050.html>.

—— (2008), 'Greenwash: BP and the myth of a world "Beyond Petroleum"', *Guardian*, 20 November <http://www.guardian.co.uk/environment/2008/nov/20/fossilfuels-energy>.

Pease, E. (1916), A *History of the Fabian Society*. New York: E.P. Dutton.

Pepper, D. (1993), *Eco-Socialism: From Deep Ecology to Social Justice*. London: Routledge.

Percy, J. (n.d.), 'Nick Origlass – a life of struggle and principle' <http://www.marxists.org/history/etol/revhist/otherdox/origlass.htm>.

Peter, L. (2009), 'EU soft on polluters, greens say', *BBC News*, 22 July <http://news.bbc.co.uk/1/hi/world/europe/8163571.stm>.

Phillips, T. (2008), 'I'd lost the strength to carry on', *Guardian*, 22 May <http://www.guardian.co.uk/environment/2008/may/22/forests.conservation>.

Prins, P., and Rayner, S. (2007), 'Time to Ditch Kyoto', *Nature*, 449: 973–5 <http://blogs.nature.com/climatefeedback/2007/10/the_wrong_trousers.html>.

Raby, D. (2004), 'The Greening of Venezuela', *Monthly Review*, November 2004.

Reitman, A. (2007), 'Climate change scepticism still exists in Brussels', *EU Observer*, 20 February <http://euobserver.com/9/23537>.

Richmond, L. (2008), 'Eco-socialism: feasible environmental solutions', *Green Left Weekly*, 26 January <http://www.greenleft.org.au/node/38929>.

Riddell, J. (2008), 'From Marx to Morales: Indigenous Socialism and the Latin Americanization of Marxism', *Monthly Review*, June.

Roberts, A. (1979), *The Self-Managing Environment*. London: Alison and Busby.

Roseneil, S. (1995), *Disarming Patriarchy: Feminism and Political Action at Greenham*. Buckingham: Open University Press.

Rotering, F. (2006), 'Ecology, Value and Marx' in *Synthesis/Regeneration*, No. 40, Summer < http://www.greens.org/s-r/40/40-20.html>.

Roy, A. (2010), 'Gandhi, but with guns', *Guardian*, 27 March <http://www.guardian.co.uk/books/2010/mar/27/arundhati-roy-india-tribal-maoists-1>.

Smith, K. (2006), '"Obscenity" of carbon trading', *BBC News*, 9 November <http://news.bbc.co.uk/1/hi/sci/tech/6132826.stm>.

—— (2008), '"Clean Development" supports dirty energy', *Green Left Weekly*, 7 November <http://www.greenleft.org.au/node/40609>.

Smollett, T. (1983), *The Expedition of Humphry Clinker*. London: W.W. Norton.

Speth, J.B. (2008), *The Bridge at the End of World*. London and New Haven, CT: Yale University Press.

Stern, N. (2007), *The Economics of Climate Change*. London: HMSO Treasury.

SV Sentralt (2008), 'The red and the green is the basis for the Socialist Left Party of Norway's SV policy', *SV Sentralt*, 30 October <http://www.sv.no/Language/English>.

Tarrow, S. (1998), *Power in Movement*. Cambridge: Cambridge University Press.

Thompson, E.P. (1976), *William Morris: Romantic to Revolutionary*. London: Pantheon.

—— (1991), *The Making of the English Working Class*. London: Penguin.

Thompson, J. and Anthony, H.M. (2009), 'The Health Effects of Waste Incinerators', *British Society for Ecological Medicine*, 11 February <http://www.ecomed.org.uk/publications/reports/the-health-effects-of-waste-incinerators>.

Thornett, A. (2010), 'Fourth International declares itself ecosocialist', *Socialist Resistance*, 5 March <http://socialistresistance.org/?p=870>.

Tockman, J. (2009), 'Independent Candidate Challenges Chilean Political Establishment', *Upside Down World*, 23 July <http://upsidedownworld.org/main/content/view/2013/1/>.

Tokar, B. (2009), 'Toward Climate Justice: Can we turn back from the abyss?', *Z Magazine*, September <http://www.social-ecology.org/2009/08/toward-climate-justice-can-we-turn-back-from-the-abyss/>.

Traub, N. and Conway, T. (2009), 'You have to be green to be red, you have to be red to be green', *Socialist Resistance*, 4 March <http://socialistresistance.org/?p=366>.

Trotsky, L. (1955), *Literature and Revolution*. New York: Russell & Russell.

Urquhart, F. and Watson, J. (2009), '£1.3 bn Highland playground for the super-rich', *The Scotsman*, 1 August <http://news.scotsman.com/internationalterrorism/13bn-Highland-playground-for-the.5514610.jp>.

Verzola, R. (2009), 'Less wants means more abundance', *Ecology, technology and social change* website <http://rverzola.wordpress.com/2009/02/26/less-wants-mean-more-abundance/>.

Vinstri Græn (2010), 'Women and Crisis', *Vinstri Græn*, 8 March <http://www.vg.is/frettir/eldri-frettir/nr/4543)>.

Wall, D. (1994), *Green History*. London: Routledge.

—— (1999), *Earth First! and the Anti-Roads Movement*. London: Routledge.

—— (2005), *Babylon and Beyond*. London: Pluto Press.

—— (2009a), 'Can the Green Left rescue Iceland?', *Red Pepper,* June 2009.

—— (2009b), 'Greens must support Visteon!', *another green world* website, 6 April < http://another-green-world.blogspot.com/2009/04/greens-must-support-visteon.html>.

—— (2009c), 'Open Source Anti-Capitalism', in Ransom, D. and Baird, V., *People First Economics*. Oxford: New Internationalist Publications.

—— (2010), 'Sinistra Ecologia e Libertà' <http://another-green-world.blogspot.com/2010/04/sinistra-ecologia-e-liberta.html>.

Weiner, D. (2000), *Models of Nature: Ecology, Conservation, and Cultural Revolution in Soviet Russia*. Pittsburgh, PA: University of Pittsburgh Press.

Whelan, D., Serafin, T. and von Zeppelin, C. (2009), 'Billion Dollar Donors', Forbes.com, 24 August <http://www.forbes.com/2009/08/24/billion-dollar-donors-gates-business-billionaire-philanthropy.html>.

White, D. (2008), *Bookchin: A Critical Appraisal*. London: Pluto Press.

Wilde, O. (1971), *The Soul of Man under Socialism*. New York: Oriole Editions.

Williams, R. (1989), *Resources of Hope*. London: Verso.

—— (1993), *The Country and the City*. London: Hogarth Press.

Wilkinson, R. and Pickett, K. (2009), *The Spirit Level*. London: Allen Lane.

Wilpert, G. (2007), *Changing Venezuela by Taking Power*. London: Zed Press.

Wilson, C. (2003), 'Indigenous People at risk as rainforests stripped bare, conference told', *Mapuche International Link*, 6 May <http://www.mapuche-nation.org/english/html/environmental/enviro-33.htm>.

Wong, E. (2008), 'In China City, Polluters See Pollution Risk of New Plant', *New York Times*, 6 May <http://www.nytimes.com/2008/05/06/world/asia/06china.html?_r=1>.

World Economic Forum (2005), 'Statement of G8 Climate Change Roundtable' <http://www.weforum.org/pdf/g8_climatechange.pdf>.

www.enviro.aero (n.d.), 'British Airways and emissions trading' <http://www.enviro.aero/BritishAirwaysEmissionsTrading.aspx>.

Index